Swing Trading for Beginners:

The #1 Step by Step Guide to Create Passive Income in The Stock Market Trading Options. Real Strategies to Create $10 000/Month Machine. Money Management & Trading Psychology

2

Please consult a licensed professional before attempting any techniques outlined in this book.

By reading this document, the reader agrees that under no circumstances is the author responsible for any losses, direct or indirect, which are incurred as a result of the use of information contained within this document, including, but not limited to, — errors, omissions, or inaccuracies.

Disclaimer

While the author has exerted the best efforts during the course of preparing and finishing this book, he makes no warranties or representations regarding the accuracy or completeness of the contents of this book. He specifically disclaims any implied warranties of merchantability or fitness for a particular purpose.

The discussions, strategies, and tips given in this book may be not be suitable for your situation. Therefore, it is best to consult accordingly with a professional as needed. The author shall not be held liable for any loss of profit or damages, including but not limited to special, incidental, or consequential damages.

Table of Contents

Chapter 1: Brief Introduction to Swing Trading

Earning profit in the stock market may be done through various means. As such, no matter what your appetite for risk and financial goals are, you would likely find one that suits you. This book primarily discusses one of these methods: swing trading.

What exactly is it?

To begin, check out the primary characteristics of swing trading:

a. Accessible
   Whether you are doing this on your own or as part of an institution, swing trading could be a profitable way to invest in the stock market.
b. Short-term
   On average, swing traders monitor the price movements of securities within a period ranging from a few days up to two months.
c. Low-risk
   Those who engage in swing trading tend to be quite sensitive about the overall condition of the market. They prefer to capitalize on low-risk opportunities, and

just try to get the most out of them whenever there is a favorable movement.

d. Adaptive
If the market is strong, swing traders either buy more or go long. However, if the market takes a downturn, they go short instead. In case the overall market is stagnant, swing traders have no problem with having to wait patiently by the sidelines.

Next, let's go over the differences between swing trading, day trading, and buy-and-hold investing. Learning how swing trading differs from other approaches would help you gain a better understanding and set more realistic expectations about investing in the stock market.

- Swing Trading vs. Day Trading
Speed best encapsulates the practice of day trading. Those who engage in this don't hold their positions overnight. Otherwise, they would put themselves at a serious risk of getting a significant portion of their accounts wiped out when the price of securities increases or decreases. As such, they monitor price movements every minute, thereby allowing them to quickly enter or exit as needed.

Day traders specialize in feeling out the volatile parts of the market. Fundamental data doesn't matter to them as much as investor psychology, which enables them to keep track of security price movements of other buyers and sellers.

Though the idea of earning profit quickly appeals to many, take note that the profit gained through this approach would be significantly reduced after taxes, commissions, and other operational costs have been deducted.

Commissions faced by swing traders tend to be high too but not as high as day trading. The longer holding period allows the fundamentals of a company to influence price movements. As such, you would have a higher potential to earn more profits by doing swing trading rather than day trading.

- Swing Trading vs. Buy-and-Hold Investing Warren Buffett famously built his wealth through this strategy. Rather than fussing about the tiny movements in market prices, he focused on studying and analyzing how things would appreciate in the years to come.

In this type of trading approach, small changes in prices are regarded as opportunities to either pick up or exit securities instead of indicators of their actual value. Because of this, buy-and-hold investors—or also known as position traders—tend to have a low annual turnover rate, averaging at 30%.

Given these passive qualities, this approach is suitable for those who aim to build or grow their wealth. Profit would take a longer time to be gained due to the nature of the investments, hence investors know that this cannot be used to generate their current income. In comparison, the more flexible swing trading approach may be a source of current income if you have enough dedication and discipline in trading stocks.

As you may have noticed, swing trading falls somewhere in the middle of buy-and-hold investing and day trading. Those who engage in it should be able to develop skills, harness techniques, and follow strategies that would allow them to grab opportunities whenever there is optimal movement in the market. They must learn how to balance being quick enough to buy or exit, thereby keeping themselves from becoming too idle while waiting for that moment.

Many investors opt for swing trading over day trading or buy-and-hold investing because it allows them to use their capital in a more efficient way and get more chances of earning higher returns along the way. However, it also opens them to costlier commissions as well as to increased volatility and risk.

Looking at the similarities and differences among the different types of stock trading approaches, you might have begun analyzing which one would suit you the best. Determining the answer to this question is one of the most important steps you need to clear in order to achieve success and maximize your profits as a stock trader. The next chapters will help you figure out if swing trading is the right fit for you.

Chapter 2: Committing to Swing Trading

Swing trading can be quite appealing for many because of the wider earning opportunities and flexible holding period that it offers to traders. However, it also requires a high degree of discipline and work ethic, as well as a moderate appetite for risk, in order to make it a rewarding venture.

Therefore, in order to assure your success, you must ask yourself first about how much of your time you could commit to swing trading. You don't necessarily have to devote your entire working day.

While many do this as their full-time occupation, there are also swing traders who only engage in this to supplement their income. Some only do this to experience the rush that you would feel while dealing with the stock market, while others start small to give themselves time to learn the ropes before committing themselves fully to the trade.

Which one of these types of swing traders do you think you would be?

Let's go over the different levels of commitment that you could give to swing trading to help you figure this one out.

- Full-Time Swing Trader

Those who intend to make swing trading their main source of income need to devote their full workday to this. However, it is not as simple as it may sound.

More often than not, people spend several months learning the ins and outs of the trade while still maintaining their current job. This involves a lot of research work to better understand what happens before, during, and after the market hours. During the course of gaining more experience, they also become more capable to monitor price movements and get their timings right.

Much of the pressure felt by full-time swing traders could be felt from the need to produce steady profits from their trades. If not handled well, some give in to the temptation of taking the risk and gambling with securities that normally wouldn't be touched by swing traders.

As a result, they experience one loss after another. Less experienced traders would react to this by countering with more trades. However, the better response would be to take a pause, reevaluate the situation, and form your next move.

- Part-Time Swing Trader
  The majority of swing traders fall under this category. They engage in this either to supplement their current income or to increase the returns on their investments. Since they are still retaining their primary job, part-time swing traders experience less stress compared to their full-time counterparts.

  Given that they dedicate fewer hours of their day to swing trading, part-timers conduct their research and analysis after their regular work hours. Their trades would then be placed on the following day. Though they may not be able to keep track of market movements throughout the day, part-time swing traders are still able to protect their investments by entering stop-loss orders as needed.

  Experts recommend going through a part-time phase first before committing fully to swing trading. Furthermore, it is highly advised to start out with a tiny part of your current portfolio. After all, you would likely make mistakes during your first few attempts. Putting a lot of capital right from the start would just make your mistakes more expensive than you could probably afford.

There are a small fraction of part-time swing traders who do it for fun. They are really not in this for the money-making potential, but rather for the "high" of making successful moves on the stock market. As such, they are more likely to ignore the established rules and strategies of swing trading, which then opens them up to more and costlier mistakes.

If you think you belong to this type of swing trader and you insist upon doing so despite the risks associated with it, then I advise you to minimize your probable losses by putting up limits upon yourself. Use only a tiny portion of your investment portfolio, and avoid tapping into your retirement funds.
Keep in mind that you would be interacting with other swing traders whose main goal is to earn a profit. That alone could put you out of the "game" faster than you are expecting.

To better set your expectations about swing trading, take a look at how a typical workday goes for Sean, a full-time retail swing trader.

A. Pre-Market
Sean starts his day early, usually at around six in the morning. This allows

him to prepare himself before the opening bell, which signifies the beginning of the trading session at an exchange.

During this period, he first makes it a point to get an overview of the market. This means catching up with the most recent development and news that may affect the market. To do this, he tunes in to a reputable news television channel, and then check out the posts on websites dedicated to monitoring the stock market, such as MarketWatch.com. From these sources, Sean takes note of the following points:

1. The general sentiment of the market
   This covers but is not limited to the important economic reports from within and outside the country, inflation, as well as currency developments.
2. The sentiment of the sector
   Sean tries to identify the hot and growing sectors that he needs to put on his list of priorities for the day.
3. Current holdings
   Updates, such as SEC filings and company earnings, are helpful when analyzing the market and making decisions later on.

Once Sean has gotten a better feel of the market, his next step is to look for potential trades for the day. Normally, a fundamental catalyst would prompt him to enter a position. In order to find one, he would employ the following methods:

a. Search for special opportunities. These may usually be found by looking at the SEC filings, and sometimes, by reading through the news headlines. To make things easier for him, Sean makes use of websites such as SECFilings.com to set up alerts for him whenever there is an SEC filing for him to check out.

Common examples of special opportunities for swing traders include mergers, acquisitions, IPOs (initial public offerings), takeovers, buyouts, corporate restructuring, and bankruptcies.

Special opportunities are attractive to swing traders because of their high profit-earning potential. However, take note that they are also quite risky so dealing with them would require a lot of careful research on your part.

If Sean is certain about a particularly special opportunity, his go-to strategy is to either buy when the majority are selling or sell when most are buying. Doing so allows him to fade the market, and capitalize when there is a reversal of the prevailing trends in the market.

b. Analyze sector plays.
Sean takes the time to seek out financial information about sectors with good performance recently. Usually, these sectors are the ones that are most popular among other traders.

However, for bigger rewards albeit higher risks, Sean would also take a look at less known sectors that are performing well. For example, compared to the fuel sector, the titanium sector may be considered as an obscure part of the industry.

In order to maximize the profits from sector plays, Sean's objective is to get his timing right and buy into the current trends, and then exit once he notices signs that the said trends are dying down.

c. Look for chart breaks.
   This involves going after popular stocks that traded a lot but are almost reaching a critical support level or resistance level.

   With the use of predictive techniques, like the Gann levels, triangles, or Wolfe Waves, Sean would be able to spot a pattern, and then buy after a breakout has occurred. However, he would then sell it again as soon as the stock reaches another resistance level.

After gathering critical pieces of information for the day, Sean would then create a watch list. Basically, the list serves as a reference about the stocks that have good potential and a fundamental catalyst.

Sean writes down his watch list on a whiteboard beside his workstation. It includes concise but important details such as the entry prices and stop-loss prices.

As a final preparatory step before the market hours begin, Sean checks his existing positions for any changes that could have happened overnight. This could easily be done by simply tapping into financial news websites that report about the stock market as well.

If there are, this might have an effect on his trading plan so he would have to take the time to analyze and adjust his strategies and priorities accordingly.

B. Market Hours
In the US, market hours begin at 9:30 AM and last up to 4:00 PM. This may vary depending on your location though, so be sure to double-check the actual market hours in your country.

Like many stock traders, Sean takes a look first at the Level II quotes in order to get a clearer idea of the price action of the stocks. In Level II, you would be able to find out the Nasdaq stocks that is sold or bought by different types of traders. You may also be able to obtain information about the direction of a particular stock that has piqued your interest.
Once Sean has found and entered a viable trade, he would start doing technical analysis in order to find an exit. His go-to technique is the Fibonacci extensions, which would be further explained later on in this book. He also tends to analyze by

looking at the price by volume and the resistance levels.

Take note, however, that Sean has already done an analysis earlier during the pre-market hours so he is just confirming again his observations based on the actual trading activities of the day. Doing so prevents him from placing trades that would be a loss or too risky for him.

Speaking of risks, one of Sean's trading rules for himself is to avoid adjusting his position just to be able to accept more risks. He would only do so if adjusting his stop-loss levels is going to lock in profits, or if the overall feel of the trading has become bullish.

C. After-Hours Market
Swing traders rarely place trades during the after-hours. After all, stocks at this point tend to be harder to sell quickly and easily without incurring a substantial loss.

As such, Sean uses this time to evaluate his performance for the day. He takes the time to carefully document his trades as well as ideas. Aside from tax purposes, doing so would allow him to reflect on the points that could be further improved upon.

To close his day, Sean reviews his open positions for the final time. He would check to significant events that may affect impact holdings, and the earning announcements made after-hours.

As you may have noticed from the above-given account of a swing trader's regular workday, it involves careful planning and thorough preparation in order to achieve success and healthy returns.

Given these, do you think you have what it takes to commit yourself to swing trading? Is this the right path for you to earn passive income and build your wealth?

If you have answered "yes" to these questions, then you have made the right decision to pick this book as your guide and companion for this particular endeavor.

There are a lot of skills involved to be a successful swing trader. However, things would be made easier if have a solid foundation for your growth and development. Learn more about the basic but important principles and terms used in swing trading.

Chapter 3: Planning Your Trade

Much like starting your own business, trading must begin with a strategic plan. This serves as both your foundation and guide to keep you from making rash decisions and costly mistakes along the way.

Failing to make a plan before engaging in swing trading would also hinder you from learning from your experiences. As a result, the progress of your growth as a trader as well as the increase of your earnings would likely not meet your expectations in the long run.

The succeeding chapters of this book shall cover how to develop and implement a trading plan. But for now, let's go over the important parts that must be included and specified clearly in your trading plan.

A. What to Trade
    The first thing to do when making a plan is to determine the type of securities that you could trade. There is a wide range to choose from, but the decision on which to select depends on various factors, including your interest, financial goals, appetite for risk, to name a few.

    To help you through this step of preparing your trading plan, I'll go over the definitions, advantages, and risks associated with the different types of securities that are popular among swing traders:

- Public Equity
  Most swing traders, especially beginners, prefer public equity—or more commonly known as stocks—because it is more familiar and easier to trade. For example, in the US, ADRs (American depository receipts) and ETFs (exchange traded funds) can be categorized under this type of securities.

  As a general rule, swing traders go after stocks that have met a particular level of volume. Doing so would keep you from making the expensive mistake of selling shares of a stock that falls below the ongoing level of volume.

  Another great thing about trading stocks is that it increases the probability of being exposed to other classes of assets. For example, you may be able to learn more about commodity gold if you are trading ETFs that are associated with gold bullion as part of its assets.

  While it is recommended for people to stick with their area of expertise in order to continually build up their skills as a trader, there is no harm in widening your knowledge about other positions that you could take.

- Commodities
  Nowadays, more and more traders are paying attention to commodities. This is brought about by their rising prices, may it be energy commodities like crude oil, or precious metals like gold.

  Profiting from commodities may be achieved by monitoring the price movements of similar stocks or ETFs. Take for example how the prices of gold bullion can be tracked by looking at the price movements of gold shares. More and more websites, such as SPDRGoldShares.com, make this easier to accomplish.

  A word of caution though. The risks and issues associated with commodities differ from stocks. Compared to equities, commodities are more volatile in terms of price and margin—among other types of risks. Therefore, take the time to research and learn more about them first before trying out your luck at trading commodities.

- Closed End Funds
  These refer to mutual funds that are mainly traded on a secondary exchange. Their prices are based on the degree of supply and demand for their shares. In comparison, open end funds have prices that are based on their net asset value, which pertains to the fund's value after the liabilities have been deducted from the assets.

  Because of its nature, closed end funds may sometimes be traded for higher or lower than their net asset value.

- Fixed-Income Markets
  Securities that are issued by different levels of government fall under this type of securities. Their values are normally dependent on the ongoing interest rates, inflation, as well as the creditworthiness of the issuing party.

  Because of the relative stability of their prices, experienced swing traders tend to avoid them. After all, they would have a higher chance of earning more profits by going after more volatile stocks or commodities.

- Currency Market

Often referred to as the foreign exchange market or simply the forex market, this is considered as the biggest global financial market. As of 2020, its overall worth is at $1.93 quadrillion. Every day, around $5.3 trillion is being traded there, making it also one of the most active financial markets in the world.

However, despite its size and volume, one limiting factor about the forex market is that it focuses on only a handful of currencies—the US dollar, the British pound sterling, the Euro, the Swiss franc, and the Japanese yen.

Beginner swing traders should also note that aside from learning how to complement the technical analysis with fundamental analysis, they must also understand how various factors—such as political stability, economic growth, and inflation—could influence the value of currencies.

- Futures Contracts
  This involves buying or selling an underlying asset with a predetermined price at a particular date in the future. There is no exchange of money between the two parties until the contract has

reached its expiration. Furthermore, a margin ranging from 5% to 10% of the total value of the contract must be posted by the traders.

Given this, extreme leverage may be imposed if the traders would like to do so. However, I discourage you from doing so because it would expose you to the risk of losing most—if not all—of your assets in the case that there is an unexpected movement in security.

B. Where to Trade
Equities, commodities, currencies, and other types of securities are traded in different financial markets. Therefore, what you decided to trade would determine where you should trade.

Financial markets can be categorized in various ways. For example, if it is based on the kinds of assets that are being traded, the markets would be classified as either traditional or alternative. Traditional markets are where financial assets like stocks and bonds are traded, while alternative markets deal with venture capital funds, fiduciary rights of real estate, investment projects, and portfolio investments—just to name a few.

Markets may also be categorized according to the phase of negotiation. Financial assets are created in the primary market, wherein the issuer could transmit them directly to traders. On the other hand, the exchange of existing financial assets that have already been issued before occurs in the secondary market.

If markets are categorized based on the assets transferred, then the sub-types would be the money market and the capital market. Assets with a term that does not exceed one year belong to the money market. Aside from money, these can be traded with any financial assets that are highly liquid and have a short-term maturity. Any asset that has medium-term or long-term maturity is traded in the capital market.

The US in particular is home to various types of financial markets that could attract all kinds of traders. For instance, stocks, ETFs, and other asset classes that are based in the US and other countries can be found in the lists of NASDAQ Exchange, NYSE (New York Stock Exchange, and AMEX (American Stock Exchange). For commodities, the CBOT (Chicago Board of Trade) is a good place to trade precious metals and major agricultural commodities like rice, corn, and wheat. Those who want to engage with crude oil, gas, and coal should check out the NYMEX (New Your Mercantile Exchange) list.

Take note, however, that stock trades are not limited to just these markets. With the rise of ECNs (electronic communication networks), traders may be able to match with big brokerage companies. Many consider this as a more efficient way to buy and sell, and sometimes, ECNs could even provide higher prices compared to ones offered by brokers.

C. When to Trade

As discussed in the previous chapter, swing traders may be classified as either full-time or part-time traders depending on their degree of commitment. This affects the timing of entering orders, which would then serve as one of the bases of the entry and exit strategies.

How exactly so?

As illustrated earlier, full-time swing traders have more time to spend researching opportunities and sector plays that are critical for analyzing the positions that they would make later on. They can also make their entries and exits at any point of the day, and take into account any changes in the price movements that have not been foreseen during the pre-market hours.

In comparison, part-time swing traders usually have other affairs to focus on during the market hours so entering orders can only be done after the market has already been closed for the day. As such, they tend to focus more on stop losses in order and limit in order to keep themselves from losing their investment.

D. How to Trade
    Your game plan for the trading opportunities you have identified is composed of various strategies for different phases of the trade.
    - Analysis
      There two primary analysis techniques employed by swing traders:
      o Technical Analysis
         Using this would enable you to analyze chart patterns, as well as apply mathematical formulas to the prices and volume of securities.

         The main advantage of this technique is that its applicability to any type of security or market. For instance, Sean uses technical analysis to quickly identify chart patterns, which would then serve as the basis for his decision on whether to buy or sell. Whether it is for stocks, commodities, bonds, or currencies, he could apply the technique as long as he could interpret the information that it would yield.

Compared to the other analysis technique—fundamental analysis—this is much quicker because you do not need to go over the details about the company's business and earnings before reaching a decision.

o Fundamental Analysis
If you want to understand why particular security is having price movements, you should use the fundamental analysis technique. This covers the fundamentals of a security or a company, including its sales and earnings.

By applying this, you would be able to determine whether the price movement is caused by fundamentals or just events in the market like the liquidation of a large mutual fund. The latter tends to be less profitable to trade in the long run, so traders want rallies and declines that are driven by the underlying fundamentals of security or a company.

Take for example the price increase of crude oil commodity. Technical analysis would likely tell you that the movement is caused by a bullish formation that has developed in the chart. When compared to fundamental analysis, this would appear like a superficial analysis of the situation, especially when the price increase is actually caused by the scarcity of the supply of crude oil in the market.

Swing traders who don't like doing fundamental analysis say that the process takes too long and may sometimes lead to inaccurate decisions. Yes, this would require you a lot of reading and research work. However, if you seek to improve your skills as a swing trader in a more holistic manner, then doing fundamental analysis could be well worth your time and effort.

As you may have noticed, technical analysis is useful when you need to determine the optimal timings for your entries and exits. Fundamental analysis, on the other hand, would help you be more prepared by telling you which direction a security or company is heading to.

- Identification and Entry
  Securities that worth pursuing may be identified through either of the following approaches:
  - Top-Down
    In this approach, the identification of opportunities starts at the market level. This would then proceed down to the industry level before ending at the company level.

    Choosing this method would influence how you enter positions. Basically, you would have to survey the general market first, then go over the industries that belong to the strongest or weakest sectors.

Ranking of securities using either technical or fundamental analysis would follow. The final step is to identify the securities that match well with your entry strategy.

○ Bottom-Up

This approach involves looking for strong securities to serve as a starting point for your analysis. The ones that belong to rising or good sectors or industries would then be chosen for entry.

People who use this approach establish a quantitative filter that shall be used to screen the securities. Usually, the screen would be based on the value or growth of the stocks at that particular time.

The securities that passed the screen would be compared against the value or growth indices of the market in order to rank them from highest to lowest value or growth. If the top ranking securities meet your entry strategy, the industries or sectors where they belong would be checked to determine if they are doing well or not. The final choice would then depend on whether you want to buy or short.

- Exit
  Inexperienced swing traders tend to focus more on their entry strategy. However, experts know that having the right exit strategy would influence when you would earn profits or losses, and when you need to redeploy your capital to a better position.

  Your exit strategy must cover the following three points:
  - When to exit to gain profit
    Since exit strategies should be based on technical data such as a trigger or catalyst, it is never recommended to listen to your gut feel even if it tells you that you are going to profit.

    A common example of a data-driven exit strategy is a stipulation wherein an exit would be appropriate only if the price has reached a certain point on a chart pattern.

  - When to exit to limit a loss

This part of the exit strategy should be based on either movement of price zones or a form of moving average. Price zones where securities have ceased falling are known as support levels. On the other hand, price zones where security prices have stopped increasing are referred to as resistance levels. Recognizing these points would be quite helpful in limiting your losses to a particular quantity only.

- When to exit if there is neither profit nor loss
  If the trade has become essentially a dead weight, many swing traders would opt to exit the position as soon as possible. Still, there are some who would wait it out first before making a decision. For example, Sean makes it a rule for him to exit only if there has not been any indication of either a profit or loss after ten days.

- Shorting
  In case of a price decline, a swing trader may still profit from this by

shorting securities. Therefore, it is wise to include this in your trading strategy.

There are two ways to go about this— either you will net long or net short. Net long means that most of the assets that you have invested into belong to the long side of the market. Conversely, net short means that the majority of your assets are on the short side instead. If there is an even quantity of long and short assets, then it is considered market neutral.

So, how exactly do you make this decision?

The answer depends on the current state of the major market index. For example, if the S&P Market Index is rising, then the majority of the swing traders are net-long. However, if it is falling, then several swing traders are net short. Market neutral swing traders can only be possible if the index says that the market is in a trading range.

- Risk Management
  Expert traders consider this as the most vital part of a trading plan. After all, a rather weak entry or exit strategy

could still lead you to earning profits if
the risk management part of your plan
restricts your losses while allowing
your profits to run.

Managing risk should be planned from
the investment portfolio down to the
individual securities. Here are the
critical points that must be addressed
in the risk management portion of your
trading plan:

o   Acceptable risk on an individual
    position
    This means you have to clarify in
    your plan the amount you plan to
    allocate for each position.

o   The acceptable risk for the total
    portfolio
    In general, swing traders set this at
    0.5 to 2 percent.

o   Achievement of proper
    diversification
    As you expose yourself to various
    types of asset classes and sectors,
    the more securities are going to be
    added to your portfolio. This
    means that you would also be
    exposed to more and different
    kinds of risks along the way.

- Long and short positions
  By combining long and short positions, you would be able to ensure that your overall portfolio would still gain something regardless of an up or down market.

- The 7 percent rule
  This trading rule states that total risk for individual positions and your portfolio should not exceed 7 percent.

- Establishment of Exit Points
  As explained earlier, exits due to profit, loss, or lack of significant market movement must be determined by technical indicators such as price zones and profit targets.

- Management Over Emotions
  Since no human being is completely devoid of emotions, a good risk management strategy must take this factor into account. Your emotions would likely be affected by the good and bad experiences as a swing trader. In

turn, they would influence how you execute your trade plan.

Those who cannot control their emotions well may find themselves ignoring or completely going against the rules that they have established for themselves. That could only lead to disastrous results.

Fortunately, emotions can be managed, and you can get better at this over time. You will find more tips on how to achieve this later on in this book.

As you may have noticed, managing risks associated with trading involves minimizing your losses at the individual and portfolio level. While you might be thinking that individual losses wouldn't hurt that much, there are certain scenarios that could significantly affect your investment.

Trading master Alexander Elder best explains this through the shark and piranha analogy. First, he described a single major loss that could inflict a "shark bite" damage to your entire portfolio. When this occurs, the value of your account would likely be significantly wiped out just because of that one particular loss.

In comparison, "piranha bites" damages happen when you encounter several small losses in a short period of time. If you would think about it, the prey of this tiny but aggressive fish would likely not die if there is only one of it. However, when a group of them attacked, then their attack tends to be quite fatal.

Applying this to your portfolio, an individual loss might not pose a serious risk to your total portfolio. Unfortunately, if you continually experience one loss after another, then they could eventually build up and cause a massive loss to you.

Given these, don't you think that spending time coming up with a solid risk management system for your trading plan is well worth your time and energy?

Now that you have a sneak peek of what is ahead of your path towards becoming a swing trader, I hope that this chapter has strengthened your resolve to pursue this endeavor.

As committed earlier, this book shall delve deeper into the concepts that you have learned so far. However, before getting into the nitty-gritty parts, it's best to familiarize yourself with the most important tips that you should keep in mind, as well as the critical mistakes that a trader might commit.

Check out the next two chapters for the top 10 things to remember and top 10 things to avoid in swing trading.

Chapter 4: Top 10 Swing Trading Tips to Remember

As mentioned in an earlier chapter, swing trading can both be a profitable and exciting way to earn money. Many regard it as a game of survival, but actually, it is more like a balancing act where you have to follow your own rules, control your emotions, and manage the risks.

To guide you on how to successfully pull this off, I'll share with you ten simple but helpful tips about swing trading. Though they may sound rather straightforward and even boring at times, these rules would keep you from losing your balance and falling off the proverbial tightrope.

Tip No. 1: Stick to your trading plan.

A trading plan serves as a general guide on how you should go about your trades. It must cover every phase of swing trading, from the research and preparation part up to your exit strategies.

However, no matter how well thought out a trading plan is, it would not be of any to use to you if you do not write it down. Traditional swing traders make sure to have a printed copy of their trading plan nearby whenever they engage with their trades.

However, more and more swing traders are opting to have a digital copy in their work computers instead. Since electronic means of trading are becoming more popular these days, this practice has proven to be more efficient and convenient for many.

A great way to ensure that you are following your trading plan is by condensing its most important points into a questionnaire form. Answering this before entering a position would allow you to analyze first in a more organized manner. It would also prevent you from giving in to temptations or your emotions, thus keeping you from making decisions that would harm your earnings or total portfolio.

For your reference, here is a sample trading questionnaire from Sean, the full-time swing trader:

- In the case of long positions, does this security belong to an industry group that is ranked within the upper 20% of the market?
- In the case of short positions, does this security belong to an industry group that is ranked within the lower 20% of the market?
- Did the volume increase according to the direction of the trade within the past few days?

- Is the direction of the overall market trends the same as the direction of the trade?
- Has there been any buy signal given for it within the past few days?
- Is the company going to announce its earnings within the next 14 days?

Sean's questionnaire may seem quite simple to answer since it only requires him to respond with either yes or no. However, each point would force him to analyze the information he has gathered so far vis-à-vis his own trading plan. In case he could not give a definitive answer, the questionnaire shall also serve as a reminder for him to conduct more research work.

Tip No. 2: Maintain a trading journal.

A trading journal is not just simply a record of all the trades you have executed. It also serves as your coach.

Since it contains important information about your trades, you can review its contents and learn more about your assumptions that have turned out well, your trading tendencies that need to either be reinforced into habits or be dropped as soon as possible and the patterns in the good and bad trades that you have entered.

By getting this general overview of your trading profile, wins, and losses, you would be able to gain self-awareness and use that accordingly to make the necessary adjustments in the way you trade. It opens up an opportunity to replicate your previous successes and points out the things you should avoid to prevent the recurrence of your mistakes.

To maintain a trading journal, you must build the habit of recording information into it after a trade has been entered. Failing to do this would likely overwhelm you later on when the data that you need to write down piles up. In the end, you might even completely give up updating your trading journal.

In general, the more details you record in the trading journal, the more useful it would be for you. The suggested content of your trading journal will be discussed further in BALIKAN Chapter _____ of this book.

Take note, however, that this also means that you need to spend more time to update it every time you make a trade. What many swing traders do to save time is to take screenshots of the trades, and add those images into the primary document or spreadsheet of their trading journal. From there, they write down other important pieces of information to complete the journal entry.

Tip No. 3: Take control of your emotions.

Emotions can ruin even the most hardworking swing traders. More often than not, those who try to make up for their losses by making more trades are not being guided by their rules but rather by their emotions. As such, what should have been just a small loss becomes bigger and bigger, some of which end up as billion-dollar mistakes.

One of the best qualities that a swing trader can have is emotional stability. Professional traders do not associate their profits or losses with their emotions. After all, whether you gain or lose is a matter of your skills and experience as a trader. They should not be regarded as a source of your happiness or a trigger for your despair.

Having control over your emotions would also help you keep your trades close to your chest. Some swing traders make the mistake of announcing the trades that they currently have, or the profits they have earned. Telling others would put you at the risk of becoming too attached to your positions. As a result, you would find it harder to make urgent but hard decisions when push comes to shove.

Emotional control is something that you have to develop over time. Don't feel frustrated if you still sometimes find yourself being subjected to the whims of your emotions. The important thing is to catch this moment as soon as possible, take a pause, and reflect on these emotions that are likely influencing your trade.

Once you become more aware of how and why your emotions are affecting your trading, you would be able to keep better track and exert more control over the emotional side of yourself.

Tip No. 4: Diversify your portfolio.

As a general rule, swing traders should have at least ten positions in different sectors in order to have a diversified portfolio. Better yet, add other asset classes as well, such as REITs (real estate investment trusts), commodities, and ETFs into the mix.

You might be wondering though why this is important in the first place.

Portfolio diversification would allow you to benefit from any kind of movement in the market. If some of your positions have become losses, you would still have the chance to offset that when your other positions earn you profits instead. Otherwise, you are going to be more exposed to the so-called idiosyncratic risk, which is brought about by having only one position from a single company.

Tip No. 5: Enter trades on a limit order.

Experts suggest entering a trade through a limit order instead of a market order. Why? Because upon execution, the price of limit orders remains the same as what you have specified. On the other hand, you do not have as much control over the price of a market order.

Limit orders also help effect the cost of market impact on you. Basically, if the order size is larger than the average volume order for the day, then your buy or sell order would have a higher chance of significantly increasing or decreasing the price of the security. In comparison, the execution of a market order might just be 2% to 5% more than the original price of the security when you made the said order.

As long as it is near the level where shares are being traded, placing a limit order may be done at any price level. It is better though to place them at a slightly lower level if you are buying, or at a slightly higher level if you are shorting.

Tip No. 6: Make use of stop-loss orders.

Some swing traders consider stop-loss orders as unnecessary once they got the hang of things. They assume that they would be able to exit a trade as soon as they observe a weak point.

However, more often than not, this is not the case for most swing traders. Because they do not recognize the purpose and importance of stop-loss orders, they end up with losses that could have been avoided in the first place.

Why are stop loss orders essential in swing trading? Basically, they reduce the risks and protect your investments in various ways, such as:

- Limiting your downside
  In the absence of a stop loss order, all of your capital would likely be your downside. To keep this from happening to you, impose an upper limit for the losses that you may encounter by placing stop loss orders.

- Helping you stay objective
  There are some traders who only make use of stop loss orders in their minds. As such, nothing or no one else could stop them from changing their predetermined stop loss order if the market begins moving against them.

  For example, your imaginary stop loss order is at $99.50. However, when the trade price dropped down to $99, you try to justify holding on to that position by telling yourself that $98.50 should be your exit point instead given the recent movements in the market. As a result of this rather impulsive change of mind, your losses would accumulate.

- Dealing with sudden, unexpected movements in the market
There are times when you need to act fast in order to save your account. If you have a diversified portfolio, that means you would have to handle around 10 different positions in a brief period of time. Without stop loss orders, you would have to do this completely on your own.

With stop loss orders in place, you may be able to take a break from swing trading whenever you need one. May it be for a vacation or to recover from an illness, you would have more peace of mind that you something would act on your positions in case the market starts acting up while you are away.

Tip No. 7: Establish your risk level.

Stop loss level is not enough to completely protect you from the volatility and unpredictability of the market. As such, all swing traders must set their acceptable risk levels for their trades.

Risk levels serve as signals for traders when the original assumptions about a particular security have turned out to be wrong. Beginner traders benefit greatly from them because having risk levels would force them to admit the mistake early on, and thus prevent them from incurring even bigger losses.

Some swing traders set the risk levels based on a certain percentage level from the entry order. However, this kind of strategy might cause automatic exits that are based on a non-existent reality on the market. For instance, if your risk level is set at 5%, then you would automatically exit a trade as soon as this level has been reached regardless of the actual daily volatility is only at 4%.

Therefore, the smarter strategy for establishing your risk levels is to base them on either the support levels or resistance levels. For example, if the support level of a stock is usually at $25, then you may assign your risk level to be $24.93. Avoid using a whole number because that would increase the likelihood of your stop loss order— which should be set at your established risk level—being the same as many others who have also placed their respective orders.

If you are not comfortable with the conspicuousness of a support level, then you could use a moving average as a basis instead. However, take note that doing so would require you more work because you need to regularly adjust because as its name implies, a moving average is in constant motion.

Swing traders who prefer trading ranges can easily identify their risk levels since all they have to identify is the continuation of an already existing trading range. Therefore, any breakout above or below the support level or resistance level indicates that it is the end of a trading range.

Tip No. 8: Assign a profit target or technical exit for your trades.

A large portion of swing traders bases their profit targets on the previous support level or resistance level. For example, they will sell 50% of a position once it has gained 5% upon its entry, and sell the remaining 50% once a 10% gain has been reached.

Another way is to base it on a technical indicator, such as a moving average or a sell signal. Doing this could be useful in generating more profits from securities that tend to trend for longer than initially expected.

Tip No. 9: Pay attention to what the overall market and industry group leads are saying.

As a general rule of stock trading, trades should match the current direction of the overall market to ensure maximum profitability. Swing traders know that if the market is in bull mode, most of their trades are in long positions. However, once it turns into the bear mode, traders switch the majority of their portfolio into short positions.

However, experienced swing traders understand that paying attention to the overall market is not enough. The performance of industry groups influences the probable returns that you could from securities.

Securities from high-performing industry groups would rise, while those from troubled industry groups would also fall. That is why when the homebuilding group was on the down back in 2007, traders had greatly profited from homebuilding companies, such as Beazer Homes USA, through shorting.

Tip No. 10: Make swing trading a rewarding experience for you.

While all traders are advised to never mix their emotions—whether positive or negative—with their business, how you feel about trading still matters in your long-term success. At the very least, you should find some form of pleasure in swing trading.

Remember, you would be spending not just your money, but also your time and energy. If you are just forcing yourself to go through it, then there is a high chance that swing trading would not be a successful venture for you. If you have realized along the way that swing trading does not exactly match your personality or goals, then you are better off trying other means of building your wealth.

Chapter 5: Top 10 Swing Trading Mistakes to Avoid

Making mistakes in swing trading is an inevitable part of the process. Even experienced traders still commit them every now and then, only to realize where they went wrong after everything has been said and done.

However, just because you didn't suffer from any consequences this time does not automatically mean that you would always be safe from loss or harm. While one or two mistakes will not lead to losing your account value, recurring mistakes would eventually catch up to you and bring significant losses to your entire portfolio.

To keep yourself from the common pitfalls of swing trading, here are 10 of the most critical mistakes that you need to avoid, and how you could arm yourself against them.

Mistake No. 1: Having insufficient capital at the start

Much like starting your own business, you need to have starting capital as part of your investment. Honestly speaking, this has to be a substantial amount because of the various costs associated with swing trading. Otherwise, your initial run would be quite hard because of the following factors:

- Trading Cost
  There is a round-trip commission charge for every security you trade. This could be quite expensive if your trading increment is relatively small as well. For example, if your trading increment is $500 and the commission charge is $20, then you need to wait for the position to increase by more than 4% to actually earn from your trade.

- Portfolio Diversification
  If you are aiming to diversify your portfolio by having at least 10 positions, then spreading a small amount of capital would make trading a lot harder for you. For instance, if your total capital is only $5,000, the average size of your trades would be only $500. That would likely not be enough to cover the amount needed to buy the shares that you are eyeing.

  Moreover, because of this, you would be forced to limit yourself to only a few positions, which in turn increases your overall risk.

Given these, how much starting capital do you actually need for swing trading? While there is no set amount that would apply for everyone, here are my suggested capital amounts for different types of swing traders:

a. For those trading for a living
If you plan to make swing trading your primary source of income, then you need to have a large starting point, not only to use for trading but also to cover your current living expenses.

Take for example Carla, who is switching from being a part-time swing trader into full-time. On average, a swing trader could make around 10% to 20% per year. Since her total monthly expenses are at about $5,000, her account value must not fall below $300,000—provided that she could achieve a 20% annual return. However, to be safe, she needs an account value of $600,000. With this, her living expenses per month would still be covered even if her annual returns are just at 10%.

To find out how much you need for yourself, take inventory of your personal expenses, and then use that as the basis for your computation about your target account value.

b. For those trading as a hobby

Normally, people who treat swing trading as a hobby have the majority of their other assets invested in a professional and diversified manner. As such, they may be able to trade about 10% to 20% of their total assets—as long as that amount is not lower than $10,000. Anything below would likely not be enough to cover the expenses associated with swing trading.

c. For those trading for their retirement fund
Building up your retirement fund usually means that you have other means of earning your current income. Given this, you could probably set your starting capital of $10,000 at a minimum—much better if you could increase it up to $20,000. With this amount, you could hold around 12 positions.

If you do not fit exactly into any of these categories, the suggested minimum capital remains to be $10,000. This amount would be sufficient to cover the swing trading costs, such as taxes, slippages, and commissions.

Mistake No. 2: Trading before earnings dates

Ideally, swing trading must be done after the company has already announced its earnings. That is why trading stocks at least one week before their earnings dates is considered a reckless move.

Earnings dates can rarely be accurately predicted. Furthermore, it is quite hard to guess whether the company has good or bad earnings for that period. Of course, you may try to gather information from the clients and suppliers of the company. Some even try to fish for information based on how the competitors of the company are doing.

Such research work normally takes a lot of time—more than what swing traders have at their disposal. Therefore, those who have a high appetite for risk tend to gamble with earnings dates especially when their gut feel tells them to do so.

This could easily be a fatal mistake for your account value. While the payout for a successful gamble is tempting, the possibility that you would encounter a major loss should be enough to dissuade you from trading before earnings dates.

Yes, there are websites now—like MarketWatch.com—which list down the upcoming earnings dates of several companies.

However, such resources cannot be used to determine the companies' actual earnings.

Mistake No. 3: Trading penny stocks

Penny stocks refer to any type of US-based stocks that are traded for a cheap price—usually less than a dollar but it can go up to $5. It attracts beginner traders because, at first glance, trading penny stocks would give you higher than average returns even if there have only been small movements in the value of the stocks.

In reality, however, penny stocks can be one of the worst addition to your portfolio. Studies show that companies that offer penny stocks are suffering from bad financial health. They could be experiencing massive losses or are burdened with so much debt that they could not afford to pay them off.

Because of the state of the companies offering them, penny stocks tend to have low liquidity. They are also highly susceptible to have price fluctuations out of the blue. Moreover, there are days when penny stocks cannot be traded at all. This would seriously hamper your ability to profit from them.

You might be thinking that penny stocks could be easily avoided since they are associated only with small or unknown companies. However, big companies like Blockbuster Inc. and Vonage Holdings had also offered them when they were in the midst of an internal financial crisis.

Mistake No. 4: Changing your reason for trading a stock

Losses are difficult to accept because it is essentially admitting that you have made a mistake. In trading, this means that rather than sell a poorly performing security, you would keep it in hopes that your initial expectations for it would be met eventually. Having this kind of mindset ignores your original objective of earning as much profit as possible from the trade while limiting the risks that you are putting yourself in.

Sean has committed this mistake during his early days as a swing trader. He bought stocks of a reputable company that is on the long side. However, shortly after this, the company has experienced a financial mishap, which resulted in a 15% decrease in the price of their stocks.

At first, Sean thought that the company would recover soon, and the price of its stocks would surely be back to 20% again. So, rather than sell the stocks, he opted to wait it out instead, even if it takes weeks, months, or even years.

Beginners tend to overlook the effect of keeping a poor-performing stock in their portfolio. Much like pruning a plant to make it grow healthier and more aesthetically pleasing, removing the problematic parts of your portfolio should be part of your strategies as you continue to diversify. This would allow you to focus more of your time, effort, and resources on trades with higher earning potential instead of being weighed down by the wrong decisions that you have made.

Mistake No. 5: Doubling down on a bad trade

Doubling down in swing trading means doubling the investment you have initially made because the trade has gone against you. This may sound counterintuitive at first, but some swing traders find this as an appealing move despite being highly risky.

Why?

Most believe that by doubling down on that particular share, you would have a chance to earn a lot more profit in case that the trade begins to move in your direction. The thing is, this strategy works a lot better for those who have long-term time horizons. They do not care much about short-term losses because they can afford to wait things out until the market conditions have become favorable for them.

In comparison, most swing traders cannot wait for years just to make a decision on whether to exit and find something else to invest in. That's why doubling down is not really recommended for those engaged in swing trading. More often than not, the risks far outweigh the expected rewards. If you have noticed that things aren't going your way within the first few days, then it is best to sell as soon as you can and minimize your losses.

Furthermore, doubling down in swing trading usually indicates that you are reacting emotionally to a probable loss. Instead of acknowledging that you have made a mistake that led to a loss, you are essentially putting more of your money into that bad trade, thinking that doing so would make things right. That is almost never the case. As discussed earlier, don't forget your original reason for trading stock.

Mistake No. 6: Going for option securities

Option securities and swing trading has never been compatible with one another. Even most professional swing traders tend to miscalculate them, thus exposing them to more risks than they can actually afford.

Why?

Because options are best left for those who need to hedge risk for speculators. They give the right to trade for a particular price at a certain time in the future. Swing traders do not benefit from this because it is nearly impossible to short-term trade options securities. You have to get the timing, direction, and magnitude of the price movements in order to be successful at it—a feat that is not achievable or realistic for most swing traders.

Furthermore, options tend to be quite expensive regardless of whether you are planning to buy or sell them. Since their spread is also wide, you would likely encounter a 5% to 10% loss in your investment if you bought them at the asking price without having the opportunity to sell them immediately.

Mistake No. 7: Being overconfident

In swing trading, too much confidence about your skills and luck often leads to arrogance. Yes, you might have gotten one win after another lately. That is certainly worthy of a celebration. However, this does not guarantee that you would always be on the winning side of things.

Believing that you would always gain from your trades would lead you to accept more and bigger risks along the way. It would also blindside you from other swing traders who may have done a more thorough prep work than you.

Such poor development leaves you open to more probable losses. Worse, rather than admitting that you have made a bad trade, you would begin making excuses, such as the marking being in the wrong instead.

Another complication of being overconfident is stunting your own growth. Some swing traders think that learning and mastering the core principles of the trade are enough to keep on achieving their targets. However, the market continuously changes so traders must keep themselves up-to-date with the latest news, theories, platforms, and techniques.

Mistake No. 8: Failing to Properly Diversify the Portfolio

There is a psychological phenomenon called familiarity bias that affects many traders. This may be observed among those who tend to invest only in companies that they have already traded with before. They get a sense of comfort and security that things would go well again because of their prior experience.

Unfortunately, familiarity bias could be quite dangerous for swing traders. This reduces the chances of diversifying your portfolio with new but promising trades. For example, you are more familiar with the technology sector so you opted to invest in different tech companies rather than branch out to other sectors.

So while you have a portfolio of 10 stocks in your account, all of them belong to the same sector. Any rise or fall in the sector would affect your entire portfolio because you have failed to completely diversify your investments. Keep in mind that the right way to diversify is to have long and short positions in various sectors and for different asset classes.

One well-known example of how this bias puts traders and investors at risk is the Enron retirement assets, which occurred in the 1990s. At that time, a large portion of their employees decided to invest their retirement assets in the energy stocks of the company. Since many opted to put everything or a majority of their retirement assets in just one place, they had placed themselves at a high risk of losing everything after the company's rapid decline.

Mistake No. 9: Placing too many trades

As described earlier in this book, swing trading falls in between buy-and-hold investment and day trading. It involves far fewer trades than day trading since it isn't concerned with every tiny movement in the stock prices. Conversely, it requires more dedication and focus than buy-and-hold investing since your sights are more on the short-term gains rather than ones that pay off after months or even years of waiting.

Achieving this balance is one of the key components to become a true and successful swing trader. While you may be tempted to keep making as many trades as you can, remember that each trade also means that you have to also invest more time, money, and effort to enter, monitor, and exit your trades. Eventually, you would also realize that you are trading stocks that move due to non-fundamental reasons, which do not lead to substantial returns.

There is no universal rule about the optimal number of trades that you could place. However, on average, swing traders hold positions for multiple days up to a few weeks.

If you notice that your holding periods is less than the average, take the time to reflect why you feel the need to make more trades than usual. Is it caused by certain events in the market, or are you becoming more impatient with your current progress? Once you have identified the probable cause, you would be able to formulate a plan to address whatever issues are affecting you.

Mistake No. 10: Failing to Follow the Trading Plan

A good trading plan is the professional swing trader's constant guide in every trade they enter, monitor, and exit. It contains the strategies and risk management measures that you have formulated for yourself. As such, it does not only lead you to gain profits but it also safeguards your capital from the ever-changing market.

Failing to follow your trading plan is tantamount to disobeying your boss at work—which in the case of swing trading: yourself. Ignoring what you have set out to do in favor of your whims at the moment would most likely hurt you in the end.

Don't think that trading plans are completely cast in stone, however. You can always make revisions to it as needed, provided that you do them after the market hours for the day has ended and only if you have good reason to do so.

In this way, you are not violating the trading plan. Instead, you are just improving upon your strategies and system based on the evaluation of your actual performance.

Chapter 6: Recommended Tools, Platforms, and Other Resources for Swing Traders

Before beginning to trade in the market, swing traders need to secure these three components: brokers, service providers, and a trading journal.

Choosing the right type of broker who is compatible with their trading plan is critical for swing traders to achieve their goals. They also need the help of certain service providers to carry out key administrative activities, such as conducting screens and analyzing charts. Meanwhile, in terms of performance evaluation and skills development, a trading journal is an indispensable tool for swing traders.

All of these points will be discussed in this chapter to give you a head-start in swing trading.

A. Brokers
   Every swing trader needs to have a broker, but not every type of broker can be helpful in executing your trades. That's why, as a beginner, you need to learn how to find and how to deal with a broker.

   First, let's go over the two major classes of brokers that swing traders tend to choose:

o Discount Brokers
This type specializes in executing trades. All you have to do is relay to them what you want to buy or sell, and they would do it for you. Nowadays, this is normally via the Internet rather than over the phone. Take note that most discount brokers offer limited services only though some do provide free services to their clients, such as bank-related services and research work.

o Direct Access Firms
If you want to have more control and trade directly with the market, you should consider hooking up with a direct access firm. Through this, you would be able to see the shares of a security that are being offered, as well as the bids for the said shares. Choosing which exchange or market maker you wish to trade with is also possible with the help of a direct access firm.

As you can see, selecting which type suits you best depends on the kind of services that you are expecting from a broker, as well as the acceptable cost of broker's commissions for you.

Full-service brokers, such as Merrill Lynch Wealth Management and Morgan Stanley, are not exactly recommended for swing traders, such as. Yes, they are more involved with their clients, and their wide range of services can be quite appealing, especially for beginners. However, all of that comes with a hefty price tag.

Furthermore, swing traders who are heavily reliant on the advice of others about which securities to trade are not exactly doing swing trading the right way. After all, having the capacity to be independent is one of the qualities of a good swing trader.

To help you find a suitable broker for you, consider looking for one at these online resources:

- o Charles Schwab
  www.schwab.com

- o E*TRADE Financial
  www.etrade.com

- o Fidelity Active Trader
  www.fidelity.com

- Interactive Brokers
  www.interactivebrokers.com

- TD Ameritrade
  www.tdameritrade.com

In order to evaluate your prospects for a broker, consider the following factors before making your choice:

- Commission Rate
  As a personal rule, the commission rate of a broker should not exceed a $10 flat fee. If the rate is per share, it should not be more than 1 to 2 cents. Anything higher than these caps would increase your target returns as well.

- Range
  For the purpose of diversifying your portfolio, look for a broker who can handle multiple types of asset classes. Take note, however, that the wider range comes with a higher price tag so keep in mind what you plan to trade and try to stick to those asset classes.

- User-Friendliness

This refers to how easy it is to use the broker's trading website or software interface. The best way to determine this is to actually try using the website or the demo version of the software yourself.

Ask yourself if entering orders can be done without much fuss. If market data gathering is one of the services of your broker, check if watching the market could be done without having to go through hoops.

o Customer Service
The broker's responsiveness to the query and concerns of the clients should be one of the most important evaluation points for you. After all, when things don't go your way in the market, you would want to have someone to help you as soon as possible.

Though you can only truly verify the quality of customer service by opening an account with the broker, you can read through the broker rankings compiled by reliable sources, such as

StockBrokers.com and Kiplinger.com, to get an idea of how well their customer service is rated by the actual clients and trading experts.

○ Bank-Related Services
These usually include the provision of a dedicated ATM card for your portfolio, online transfer of assets, and writing of checks from your account. If such services are vital to you, then your ideal broker should be able to them as well.

○ Documentation and Analysis
A broker who can handle these for you would be a great time-saver, especially for tax-related paperwork. Beginners would also benefit from portfolio analysis done by professional brokers, especially since it usually takes some time to understand the various indices that are used to compare your performance.

○ Amenities
Common amenities offered by brokers to their clients are

research services, stock reports, and charting programs. With regards to research, swing traders don't really avail them because those are generally about long-term trading opportunities, which are not really that useful for swing trading.

Once you have chosen your broker, your next step is to open an account. There are 4 major types to choose from: cash account, margin account, traditional brokerage account, and retirement account.

Which one should you choose?

Basically, your choice depends on what you intend to do. For example, do you plan to borrow your trading money from the broker?

Cash accounts will limit you to the amount of cash that you currently have in your account. On the other hand, margin accounts enable traders to borrow money to invest from the brokers.

Take note, however, that the amount of money you could borrow cannot exceed the amount of cash you have in your margin account. That means if you have

$20,000 in your margin account, the most you could borrow from the broker for your trade is $20,000 as well.

Beginner traders should avoid opening margin accounts. Investing the money that is technically not yours tends to lead to gambling with riskier securities and strategies. As much as possible, stick with trading the current assets that you own rather than exploring the market with money that isn't yours.

If you are after a convenient access to your money, then traditional brokerage accounts would give this to you. However, particularly in the US, choosing this type would turn your profits into taxable income unless the IRS (Internal Revenue Service) officially classifies you as a full-time trader.

You may be able to avoid taxes by opening a retirement account, but that would seriously limit the amount of money you could deposit into the account per year, as well as the amount of money that you could withdraw without triggering the penalties.

B. Service Providers

Traders rely on various types of service providers, especially those that offer access to a key database or charting. Here are some of the most useful ones that you should do business with as a swing trader:

- o Technical Software
  Good charting software is an essential companion of every swing trader.

  If you plan to trade intraday, then the software should be able to incorporate quotes and charts that are updated on a real-time basis. However, if you are a part-time swing trader who only enters orders after the market has closed for the day, then a real-time chart is not important to have.

  To guide you on finding a technical software that is easy to use, check out the charting services offered by the following popular service providers:

  - Active Trade Pro
    www.fidelity.com

  - E*Trade Pro
    www.etrade.com

- TradeStation
  www.tradestation.com

- ○ Database
  The newspaper "Investor's Business Daily" is a great resource for those seeking fundamental data about a large collection of stocks. The finance section of Reuters.com also offers data about the overall market, as well as comparisons between one company to another.

Staying up-to-date with the latest financial and market news may also be possible through the help of news-focused service providers. While you can set alerts in the trading software you are using to inform you of the changes happening in securities, keeping tabs on what is occurring in the market is essential for making smart trading decisions.

Here are a couple of recommended sources of financial and market news:

- ○ MarketWatch
  Introduced by the Dow Jones & Company, this website is useful in

monitoring the pulse of various markets. Aside from the latest news about the stock market, financial updates, and business developments, it also offers financial advice to its users, as well as stock market quotes.

o   Investing.com
    For real-time news, charts, and an economic calendar, visit this website on a regular basis. It is also known among traders for its various tools and calculators, as well as in-depth posts about commodities, currencies, futures, and options, just to name a few.

o   Real Vision TV
    First things first: to get full access to information from this source, you need to pay for a subscription. It does offer a free 1-week trial for only $1 so that you can decide if this is their content that is useful for you as a swing trader.

    To give you a better idea of what to expect, here is a quick rundown of what to expect from this website:

- Videos of talks and interviews done by experts in trading, investments, and economics
- Popular topics covered include interest rates, currencies, and equity markets.
- Provides access to debates among experts regarding new issues or innovations in the trading world
- Offers content for any type of trader

For traders who want to engage with the forex market, there are plenty of dedicated resources that you can tap into in order to get a better idea of what's going on there. Here are some of the most recommended resources for both beginners and more experienced traders alike:

- FXStreet
  A large portion of forex traders considers this as the top resource when it comes to reliable news and updates. This website covers a wide range of topics and currencies, including controversial cryptocurrencies.

Much of the articles posted here are from the FXStreet team itself. However, you may also find every now and then some content made by trading brokers and even banks every now and then.

o Forex Factory
This website provides real-time forex news that is aggregated from other news sites. As such, you may expect to get more comprehensive updates about foreign currencies from their posts.

The tagging system of Forex Factory is also incredibly useful, especially for swing traders. High-impact news posts are marked in red, the medium-impact ones are in orange, while the low-impact updates bear the color yellow.

o DailyFX
This is one of the most popular websites among forex traders because of its excellent posts about market analysis. Furthermore, they are known for supporting their posts with a technical

analysis, which you could use as reference points for your trading strategies.

DailyFX also touches on whether the forex market is in bull or bear mode. They do this by sharing the percentage of traders who are either buying or selling on certain currency pairs.

- BabyPips
  Beginners would benefit greatly from this website since they are more known for producing educational posts about the forex market. They also provide a forum so that traders could interact and exchange their opinions and advice with one another.

  Aside from educational materials, BabyPips also post forex articles, though the majority of what they release are based on the US dollar. Aside from articles, the website also posts a forecast for the week every Monday, while their Fridays are reserved for the weekly review of various currencies.

A word of caution though. Not all service providers for traders can be beneficial for you. Some may even cause havoc in your portfolio and prevent you from making good trades.

For example, avoid checking message boards about stock investments, such as those found in Reddit forums. While it is tempting to connect with other traders, the information available there is unreliable and often based on subjective experiences that would likely not apply to you as well.

Newsletters that give out recommendations on which stocks to buy or sell are not exactly helpful for traders in general. Yes, they might be market experts who really do know what's going on. However, simply listening to their suggestions and acting upon them might cause you to follow blindly a piece of advice that will ultimately be bad for you.

In the long run, it is better for traders should learn how to think independently. You may refer to newsletters if their content deals more with the overall picture of the market or an industry-level analysis. That could actually serve as your guide when making your trades later on.

C. Trading Journal
Continual improvement is one of the keys to becoming a successful swing trader. However, honing your skills without basing them on your previous performance is like going on a journey without any map or guide. You would likely make the same mistakes over and over again, and as the saying goes, that's insanity.

One of the best tools a trader should have in order to achieve continually is a trading journal. It is basically a record of every single trade that you have made.

A good journal entry is concise but meaningful in the sense that by just reading through it, you would be able to understand the following:
- o how you found the trade in the first place
- o the name and a brief description of the position that you have traded
- o triggers that made you enter that trade
- o technical indicators that you have gotten from the charts that you have reviewed before making your entry

- the reason for your exit, preferably accompanied by a relevant chart of the given security
- the return rate after you have made your exit

You are free to add more elements to your trading journal, as long as you could commit to updating your entries in a timely manner. For example, some traders prefer to add the size of the position and chart of the overall market so that they could refer back to these data points before making decisions about entering a trade. However, that would naturally increase the amount of time and effort that you need to exert in order to create a journal entry.

Therefore, the key to successfully keeping a trading journal is to balance between being informative and being convenient. During your first days as a swing trader, try out different formats for your journal entries until you find one that would be useful and sustainable for you.

Chapter 7: Developing Your Trading Approach, Style, and Strategy

Your approach, style, and strategy as a trader would influence how you find and handle promising trading opportunities. In this chapter, you will learn about the two general scope approaches—top-down and bottom-up, the two main trading styles—discretionary and mechanical, and the two primary trading strategies—technical analysis and fundamental analysis. Your main goal at this point is to determine which of these would suit your interests, preferences, and skill level.

A. Top-Down Approach vs. Bottom-Up Approach
If you plan to follow the top-down approach, you need to find securities with good earning potential by starting at the macro level and industry group level and then narrowing it down to the company level.

However, if you look for promising securities first before screening them according to the performance of the respective industry groups where they belong to and macro-level fundamentals, you are doing the bottom-up approach.

You might be wondering if one of these approaches is better than the other. Most trading experts say no, but you do have to select only one of the two instead of trying to do both. Since either approach is useful for swing trading, your choice would all boil down to your personal preferences and skill level as a trader.

Take note that you have to combine a top-down approach or bottom-up approach with any trading strategy that you would decide on for yourself. For example, those who choose the top-down approach should analyze industry chart patterns to recognize which of the stocks are strong. Further investigation about the companies' fundamentals must then be conducted to determine which one of them must be bought or shorted.

On the other hand, a bottom-up trader would greatly benefit from fundamental screens to find undervalued securities. Once found, they can then analyze chart patterns to verify if those securities are strong or weak.

B. Discretionary Style vs. Mechanical Style
    Traders who evaluate the potential of trade against their trading plan follow the

discretionary style. Whether they use technical analysis or fundamental analysis to do so isn't the main point. Discretionary swing traders could use either or both strategies as long as their evaluation criteria are based on the predetermined trading plan.

However, swing traders following this style are not exactly bound by the rules that are set in the trading plan. They still factor in their previous experiences and gut feel at times to finalize their decision about a particular trade.

Because of this, the main advantage of the discretionary trading style arises when analyzing a set of data from another perspective that could not be captured by most trading software programs. This is a double-edged sword though.

Since traders themselves decide on whether to take or pass on trades, there is a chance that emotions might come into play, thus violating one of the most important rules of trading. Those who succumb to this and become emotionally attached to their trades usually end up ignoring their trade plan altogether.

To avoid such shortcomings, consider following the mechanical trading style instead. To do this, you have to use strategies that could be executed by a trading software program. These may include technical indicators, as well as fundamental data points, such as the company's rate of sales growth.

Once the information has been inputted, the software would process it based on other historical market data. The output will then be analyzed by the swing trader to determine if the strategy that has been tested by the software is worth pursuing.

As you can see, the mechanical trading style removes as much human interference as possible. The trader's inputs will be limited to the capital allocation for the positions, the signals for entry, and the rules for an exit. As for the rest of the analysis, the computer program shall handle them on its own.

Unfortunately, there is no trading software that has been proven to capture all the events or conditions that could arise from the trades. Furthermore, a lot of swing traders do not like relying completely on computer programs to evaluate their trades. As such, the majority still prefer using the discretionary style to evaluate the potential of trades.

No matter which approach or style you decide to follow, the two main trading strategies may be used to examine securities. Swing traders, especially beginners, mostly lean towards technical analysis than fundamental analysis.

Why?

The answer can be summed up in two words: "convenience" and "objectivity".

Technical analysis does not require as much effort as fundamental analysis, wherein you would have to consider the companies' industry dynamics, management structures, competitors, just to name a few. All these pieces of information, however, can still lead to an inaccurate conclusion because they are less subjective compared to chart patterns and technical indicators.

Fundamental analysis is far more popular among buy-and-hold investors, too. After all, there is no assurance that the shares of an undervalued company would rise in value within the next few days. In some cases, it can take up to months or even years before a reasonable return can be achieved.

Still, some trading experts recommend combining the two strategies in order to come up with a more holistic understanding of the trade. Each method has its own drawbacks that may be addressed by the other. Fundamentals could also provide more context to technical indicators, thereby allowing traders to understand what is driving the price movements in the market.

You don't necessarily have to integrate technical analysis with fundamental analysis though, especially if you are just doing it for the sake of it. Remember, you should base your decision about your trading strategy on your personal preference and skills.

To help you determine if technical analysis or fundamental analysis is suitable for you, let's go over each strategy in greater detail.

- Technical Analysis
  Though its name may sound intimidating for beginner traders, this strategy can actually be as simple as interpreting chart patterns to identify the direction of securities. If you could learn how to do this, then you may be able to work up your way to more complex analysis, like Intermarket evaluations, later on.

  In general, traders use technical analysis to determine the following points:

- If the security is trending or in a trading range
- If the market will be in a bull or bear mode and how that would affect the security
- If the buyers or sellers are in control of the market
- If the controlling party's strength is increasing or decreasing
- If a reversal or failure is imminent
- The entry and exit signals to watch out for

Given these, here are the main advantages of technical analysis:

- Can be used to quickly analyze an individual security
- It may be applied in a consistent manner across different markets and time
- Can indicate the level of rationality of buyers and sellers
- It may be used to determine the support levels and resistance levels that would signal entries and exits
- Minimizes the subjectivity of the traders when analyzing charts

On the flip side, here are the drawbacks of technical analysis:

- o Always assumes that the market is right
- o Does not factor in the fundamentals of security and major events of the company
- o Includes irrational traders in the analysis

Despite these shortcomings, technical analysis remains to be the preferred choice of a large majority of swing traders. It has been proven to be effective in providing insights about how prices would move in the future.

But how does this strategy actually work? In general, the technical analysis relies on two components: charts and technical indicators.

Analyzing securities using chart patterns is appealing for many because it is relatively easy to do. Many traders, even those who primarily rely on fundamentals, refer to stock charts before buying. There are several types of charts that swing traders can use, but the most popular ones are the bar charts, candlestick charts, and line charts.

Technical indicators, on the other hand, are primarily used by traders to determine the right direction for them to take. To use them, you must first apply them to security prices before analyzing the strength of particular security against the overall market.

These two aspects of technical analysis will be discussed further in later chapters of the book.

- Fundamental Analysis
This strategy is mostly concerned about the value of the company compared to its peers, as well as the company's growth rate and returns. If traders know these data points, they would be able to have a better idea about the reasonable prices for the shares of a particular company.

For instance, traders are more willing to pay more for the shares of a company that has higher earnings. They rationalize this by expecting that the company's future earnings would also be good.

Swing traders don't usually use this strategy because such expectations may take a long period of time to be realized. Still, this method does have its own merits—some of which address the shortcomings of technical analysis.

- Provides an estimate of a company's intrinsic value instead of just its market value
- Takes into account the effects of industry and market events that could affect security prices
- Allows assumptions that the market could be wrong sometimes

As you can see, most of the advantages of fundamental analysis revolve around its ability to determine the actual worth of a company. That could be quite useful for swing traders because, as explained earlier in this book, it tells them if the price movements in the market are actually driven by the company's fundamentals rather than just by mere market noise.

On the other hand, the drawbacks of fundamental analysis are mostly due to its nature as a trading strategy.

- More subjective because it hinges upon the ability of the trader to interpret the information at hand
- Cannot be used to determine where assumptions went wrong upon exiting a trade
- Tends to be less accurate when used for short-term analysis

About the last point, swing traders who use fundamental analysis make up for this by analyzing catalysts—or the internal or external events that could influence the short-term price movements as well as the market value of a company's shares. Examples of catalysts are corporate mergers, earnings dates, acquisitions, and the release of new products.

Given what you have learned in this chapter, start reflecting on which of the various types of trading approaches, styles, and strategies. Don't worry though if you cannot make up your mind yet. The next chapters shall continue the discussion about how they work as a means of analyzing the market.

Chapter 8: Getting to Know Stock Charts

Traders use charts to study the relationship between the price and volume. Though the price is usually considered more important when making a decision, the volume demonstrates the commitment of buyers and sellers. As such, understanding how each chart component affects one another could tell you when to enter or exit a trade.

While reading charts is an easy skill to gain, it does require you to learn not just one type of chart but at least the four main types: bar chart, candlestick chart, line chart, and P&F (point and figure) chart.

A lot of swing traders favor using the candlestick chart because they find it to be the most informative type. They show patterns that can be used to determine your entries and exits. However, line charts and bar charts are considered as the most commonly used ones, while the less common P&F charts can be quite useful in filtering out unnecessary data points.

It is never wise to just rely on a single type so let's go over each type of chart and how they are used in technical analysis. Discussions of how to interpret the chart patterns shall be covered in the next few chapters of this book.

o   Bar Chart

Bar charts show a security's open, high, low, and close. As such, it is also known as the OHLC bar chart. It may be used to showcase information on an hourly, daily, weekly, or monthly basis.

A standard bar chart is composed of two horizontal lines that protrude from the bar signals. The one on the left is the opening price of the security, while the one on the right indicates the closing price. Meanwhile, the top and bottom of the bar show the highs and lows of the period.

- Candlestick Chart
  Just like a bar chart, this type also indicates the open, high, low, and close of securities, but because of its two components—the real body and the shadows—it presents information in a clearer manner. The real body is the range that exists between the open and close, while the shadows demonstrate the price movements.

  If the closing of security is higher than its opening during that particular period, the real body tends to be light in color. On the other hand, the body becomes dark in color if the closing is lower than the opening. In case that the security opens and closes at the same level, the body becomes a horizontal line only, though shadows in the upper and lower parts remain.

o Line Chart
The lines in this chart show the connections of closes from a certain period to the next. While many use this because it is simple to understand, a line chart does not actually say much even though it does highlight the closing price for the day—which, for many, is one of the most important pieces of information to remember.

First, it cannot be used to find out where the security has opened for the given day since its focus is on the closes. The highs and lows of each period cannot also be determined by looking at a line chart.

o P&F Chart
This chart type can filter out market noise—which refers to price movements that are not really important for traders. However, their main drawback can be seen when the given security did not have any significant price movements for several days.

A P&F chart is composed of Xs and Os. Rising price movements are indicated by a column of X's, while O's show falling price movements. Its ability to screen information is possible because new X's and O's can only be added to the chart if the price movement meets a pre-determined amount.

As mentioned earlier, charts depict the relationship between price and volume. However, rather than just showing a single point, charts can actually showcase the four different phases of the natural cycle of securities.

Learning how this cycle goes is important because the different phases denote the need for a different trading strategy. Therefore, let's take the time to discuss each phase and how you could recognize them in charts.

A. Accumulation Phase
This is normally the longest phase-out of the four. At this point, there is no meaningful movement in the price of a security. As such, you will not see any significant rise or fall, just sideway movements through time.

During this phase, a balance between the supply and demand is being maintained most of the time. Smart money—which pertains to money that is being invested by people who have extensive knowledge about the industry—tend to gather more shares of undervalued security.

Because almost everyone in the market agrees that the price of the security is accurate, the volume during the accumulation phase is typically light. Prices cannot be pushed further than a ceiling—or a resistance level—by the buyers, and cannot be pushed lower than a floor—or a support level.

Ceilings and floors cannot be predicted accurately, but they can be easily spotted in price charts, where they are shown as price levels that securities couldn't rise above or fall below.

B. Expansion Phase
Also referred to as the markup phase, this is best described as a period where prices begin to increase. Because of this, swing traders who trade trends take long positions as soon as securities reach this phase. This can last for multiple days or even weeks, so the earlier you buy the more opportunities to profit you will get.

Stocks usually expand when the outlook for the earnings of a company is expected to improve. For example, the successful launch of new iPhones of Apple has led to a steady rise in their share prices.

You can easily see in a chart if security has truly reached the expansion phase—that is the volume becomes strong. If the volume is weak, that means that the increase will be short-lived due to the lack of conviction from the buyers. This indicates that the security will likely fall back to its price when it was in the accumulation phase.

C. Distribution Phase
This phase indicates that the share prices have started to even out again. Experienced traders know that this is a signal to either exit their long positions or enter short positions.

On the other hand, beginner traders are often fooled into buying during the distribution phase because they have mistaken it for the accumulation phase. This usually occurs when the news of a good investment opportunity only reached them after everyone else also knew about it. In reality, the expansion phase is already nearing its end, and share prices are about to drop again instead of continually rise.

To differentiate the accumulation phase from the distribution phase, you must:
- o Observe if there is mark-up or mark-down before the phase that you are looking at. The former denotes a distribution phase, while the latter indicates that it is an accumulation phase.
- o Check out the fundamentals of security. Normally, if the fundamentals are on the strong side, then that is an accumulation phase.

Other signs of a distribution phase may be given by the companies themselves. For example, if they know that their shares are overpriced, they tend to open to the public a secondary offering of new stocks.

D. Contraction Phase
A security's natural cycle ends with the contraction phase, or also known as the markdown phase. This is depicted in charts as a series of highs and lows that are lower than the other three phases. As

such, sellers who short benefit the most at this time.

Be extra cautious with securities that have entered this phase. Many traders, especially beginners, make the mistake of buying securities that have fallen in price but have not yet reached their true bottom.

The price decline does not happen in a steady fashion. You might be thinking that security has already hit its lowest point, only to realize later on that it could drop to a new low.

Why would buyers even consider such securities in the first place?

Known by many as "bottom fishing", this phenomenon stems from the idea that you will be profiting from the all-time-low prices, especially once the cycle renews itself. Plus, there is a certain psychological pleasure experienced when you buy something that used to be more expensive for a much lower price now.

Unfortunately, the rise of securities happens at a slower rate than their fall. A security may lose its gains for the past months in just a matter of days, but as discussed earlier, the accumulation phase lasts for a long period of time.

Remember as well that security prices rise due to the greed of buyers, but they decline when fear starts to set in. Since fear tends to be stronger than feelings of want, it affects traders at a much faster pace. As a result, fear-stricken traders sell as fast as they could.

Security rallies during the contraction phase is a normal movement, but it is not a sign for traders to buy. Instead, they are signs for the short sellers' entry points.

The best way to go about the contraction phase is to wait until it is over. Better yet, before making your move, wait until the security is either in its accumulation phase again or is about to enter the expansion phase. By doing so, you would be able to ensure that your next trades will go along the direction of the overall market.

Now that you have a better idea of what charts are in the world of trading, let's proceed to the next chapter and discuss how to make sense of chart patterns.

Chapter 9: Understanding Chart Patterns and Trendlines

To be perfectly honest, chart patterns have received skepticism from the academic side of trading. After all, seeing shapes and sequences can be a subjective observation, especially when the reader isn't even quite sure if the pattern actually exists or if it is just a product of one's overactive imagination.

Nonetheless, many trading experts consider the skill of reading chart patterns as essential to be successful in whichever type of trading you plan to engage in.

While computer programs may be created to look out for patterns, it is quite difficult to establish systematic and consistent rules for them to follow. Therefore, experienced traders know that to reduce the probability of making a purely subjective reading of a chart, they only seek out the five major patterns: cup and handle, Darvas box, gaps, head and shoulders, and triangles.

Yes, other chart patterns exist, but these five types are the most commonly seen and used by traders. To better understand how they could help you interpret a chart, let's go over each major type of pattern.

A. Cup and Handle Pattern

This chart pattern indicates that the security is on the verge of a rising movement as the shares continue to accumulate. Since it is technically a continuation formation, it must be followed immediately by an uptrend.

The formation of this pattern happens once the shares start to rally to form a peak. Then, shares will be brought down by 10% to 20% from the peak by sellers either due to a fundamental or technical reason.

Inexperienced traders who bought shares during this time would think they have made a mistake. As such, they usually want to sell as soon as they have reached a breakeven.

The thing is, the shares they bought near the peak would give them the opportunity to do so once the said shares begin to rally again back to the peak. After the mass selling of the inexperienced traders, a resistance level will be created, thus preventing the shares to go higher than the current peak.

Still, the shares do not drop down to the previous low because smart money would start to accumulate at a small discount. At most, the fall of shares is going to be around 5%.

The shares will then have a second attempt to break through and surpass the peak. If the volume is sufficiently heavy, the full cup and handle pattern would be realized.

Take note that the cup and handle pattern is not considered to be as reliable as the head and shoulders pattern. There are times when it would show a false breakout instead.

To keep yourself from falling into this trap, double-check the current performance of the overall market and industry group to where the security belongs to. If the overall market and industry group is strong, then the breakout is more likely to be genuine. Otherwise, there is a high probability that cup and pattern formation will fail.

B. Darvas Box
This chart pattern is introduced by Nicholas Darvas, a professional ballroom dancer who developed his personal trading system by reading investment books during his spare time. His development as a trader over the years

allowed him to turn $25,000 to over $2.2 million within a span of 18 months.

As the name implies, the Darvas box is used to show that the price of securities usually trades between the support level and resistance level before passing through a certain price level and then either rallying or falling from then on. If you would remember from the previous chapter, this indicates the securities are in their accumulation phase.

Through this rectangular-shaped pattern, Darvas highlighted the following observations. A support level indicates the price point wherein buyers decided to buy shares, thus keeping the price of the security from decreasing. On other hand, a resistance level shows where sellers started to sell shares, thereby preventing the security price from increasing. In line with these rules, any security that doesn't follow this would be automatically ignored by Darvas.

Once a security has been identified to be trading between the support level and resistance level, the waiting game would commence for Darvas. He would bide his time until the security had breached through the upper band with a heavy volume.

At that point, Darvas would buy the security. A stop-loss order will be placed under the support level of the rectangle. In case that a new rectangle would appear because the security had risen, the stop loss level will be adjusted accordingly to the new support level indicated by the rectangular pattern.

The Darvas box may be useful for short sellers, too. Basically, all they have to do is reverse the original rules for this chart pattern. If a security that has been trading between the two levels breaks through and goes below the support level, then it is time to short.

A stop loss level will be established on top of the said support level, but if a Darvas box forms below that, they would also move the stop loss to the upper part of the new resistance level.

C. Gaps
   Breaks in price continuity may be represented by gaps in the chart. For instance, the trading range of a particular

security is in the $24 to $25 range, but with a gap up to $30.

There are four types of gaps to look out for:

    a. Common Gaps

These are gaps up or down in prices that appear and then disappear when the gap becomes filled in after a few days. When this occurs, the price just returns to its original level before the gap has appeared.

Common gaps are essentially meaningless to traders, and therefore should not be used as a signal to trade. Their volume is normally light, so they do not reflect the convictions of either buyers or sellers.

    b. Breakaway Gaps

If there are major changes happening in the security, a breakaway gap will appear. You can easily spot them because their volume is so heavy that it is usually twice the average daily volume. The percentage also increases or decreases significantly.

A congestion period precedes the occurrence of a breakaway gap. During that time, the price level where the security has been trading at for weeks or months suddenly shoots up or down in just one day. This rather violent movement reflects how the value of a security has changed among investors.

Swing traders should still exercise caution when it comes to breakaway gaps. After all, many things could still happen after it has occurred. However, once you have confirmed that the breakaway gap is true, you should try to buy or sell as soon as you can.

c. Continuation Gaps
    As the name suggests, this type of gap indicates the continuation of the previous trend while security is in either an uptrend or a downtrend.

    Some swing traders use continuation gaps as a reference point in estimating how far the price levels of a security will move. By looking at how much the price has appreciated or depreciated prior to the continuation gap, they try to project how far the trend will go from then on.

Unfortunately, experts say that doing so could be somewhat subjective. So rather than this, they suggest analyzing what will happen if you buy or sell depending on the direction of the gap.

Then, check if whether or not shares will return to fill that gap after you have placed a protective stop loss within the said gap. If they did not, then what you have there is a true continuation gap.

d. Exhaustion Gaps
This gap signals the end of a trend. Some mistake this for a continuation gap. However, as explained earlier, shares do not fill a continuation gap, but they do for an exhaustion gap. Ultimately, this type of gap does not prompt any action from a swing trader.

D. Head and Shoulders Pattern

This is widely considered as one of the most reliable chart patterns among traders. Even the Federal Reserve Bank of New York agrees with this observation. In one of their articles entitled "Head and Shoulders: Not Just a Flaky Pattern", they stated that this pattern has repeatedly shown a certain level of being predictive, thereby allowing its users to earn profits in some markets.

The head and shoulders pattern signals the end of an uptrend. It is characterized by three "hills". The left and right sides are almost of the same height, while the middle hill is the tallest, thus giving the pattern its recognizable head-and-shoulder shape.

E. Triangle patterns
This chart pattern demonstrates the competing relationship between the buyers and sellers. Depending on the situation in the market, one party would have the upper hand over the other—though there are still times when both are in a stalemate.

Given this, triangle patterns highlight the so-called measurement movements in the market. This may be used by traders to gain an estimate of how far the current trend will go after it has broken out of the triangle formation. Let's discuss how you could do that by going over the three main types of triangles:

a. Ascending

This triangle pattern forms when the buyers are strong and steady while the sellers continually get weaker.

In this scenario, the buyers push the shares back every time the sellers try to bring the prices down. This attempt to push back the prices, however, always ends up higher than the previous one. If the buyers continue to overwhelm the sellers, the security will then break in an upward manner.

To measure how far the prices will move upon breaking out, add the height of the triangle—or the vertical part that exists between the support levels and the resistance levels—to the breakout price level of the security.

b. Descending

As its name implies, this is basically the direct inverse of the ascending triangle. Sellers are able to maintain their strength as buyers grow steadily weaker.

In charts, you will see these dynamics as a series of falling prices that are followed by rallies that end in lower peaks than the previous one. At some point, the buying pressure will lose power, thereby giving way to a downward break of prices.

Price movements after this breakout may be determined by deducting the height of the triangle from the breakout price level.

c. Symmetrical
This pattern appears if the buyers and sellers are evenly matched. The rallies end at a lower point than the previous one, while the declines stop higher than their past troughs.

In such cases, there is no easy way to tell which party will win. However, you may expect the price movement to continue along the direction that the trend has taken before the symmetrical triangle has appeared.

Estimating the price movement may be done by either adding to or subtracting from—depending on how the prices break—the height of the triangle from the breakout level.

Regardless of which type of triangle pattern appears on the chart, keep your eye on the actual volume of the breakout to determine if the breakout is true or false.

In terms of trading, it is best to stick with either ascending or descending patterns since you are certain about which direction the breakout will be taking. Symmetrical triangles are riskier, so avoid them as much as possible.

The patterns that appear in candlestick charts are quite distinctive so they deserve a separate section. There are several variations to look out for, but the following four pattern formations are the ones considered by many traders as the easiest to recognize and the most accurate in terms of signaling changes or continuation of trends.

1. Hammer

This signifies the bottom of a given trend because it appears at the of a downtrend. This means that after a security price has been opened, the sellers in the market have brought it down. Buyers, on the other hand, should have recouped a large portion of their losses by the end of the day.

The real bodies of the hammer are small in the upper part of a candlestick bar. Meanwhile, their lowers shadows are long, and if they have any, their upper shadows are small.

Hammers must always have a confirmation. It is better to see one that goes even lower than the latest price action. Otherwise, you may disregard that hammer for being an unreliable indicator of the trend's bottom.

Another way to confirm hammers is through volume. True hammers are formed on heavy volume. Those that don't, cannot be considered genuine.

2. The Hanging Man
   Though the name sounds intimidating, this chart pattern is quite bland. Though it looks similar to a hammer, it appears at

the end of an uptrend instead of a downtrend.

To confirm if what you are seeing is a genuine one, check if it emerged on heavy volume and if it's high will not be breached through by the subsequent price action. If these conditions are not met, then the signal you have observed is false.

3. Bullish Engulfing Pattern
   This chart pattern involves two candlestick bars each. A bullish engulfing pattern may be observed if the opening of a candlestick bar is lower than the closing of the previous candlestick bar and if the closing of that same candlestick bar is higher than the opening of the previous candlestick bar.

   Looking at this in a chart, you will notice how it starts with a candlestick bar with a small real body. This is then followed by another candlestick bar that has a body that engulfs the real body of the previous candlestick bar.

   What does this pattern exactly mean though?

A bullish engulfing pattern signifies a big "defeat" for the bears. By the time the second candlestick bar opens, sellers are already attempting to push down the prices until they become lower than how much they were when they closed the previous day.

However, this is thwarted when the buyers start buying in large quantities. As a result, the buyers manage to change the direction of the trend, they are able to increase the prices even higher compared to the previous day. All in all, it's an overwhelming victory for the buyers that day.

4. Bearing Engulfing Pattern
   Like its counterpart, this pattern also involves two candlestick formations. The difference is that it occurs at the end of uptrends, thus indicating where important reversals happen.

   The real body of the first candlestick bar is smaller than the second one. This reflects how the opening of the second candlestick is higher than the closing of the first candlestick, and how the closing of the second candlestick is lower than the opening of the first candlestick.

As always, remember to wait for confirmation first before proceeding with your plan to short a bearish engulfing pattern. There are some cases wherein this formation does not lead to decreased prices. You will know that you are dealing with a true bearish engulfing pattern if the prices declined after it occurred and it didn't surpass the bearish engulfing bar's high.

5. Morning Stars and Evening Stars
   Both of these chart patterns are comprised of three candlestick bars. What distinguishes them from one another is where they can occur.

   Basically, a morning star signals the end of a downtrend and the start of an uptrend. This reflects how the bears are in force before the reversal happened. Meanwhile, an evening star represents the end of an uptrend and the beginning of a downtrend. This demonstrates the last moments of the bulls before the change in trend has taken place.

   How does each of these patterns appear on charts?

A morning star is made of the following:

- First Candlestick Bar
  Has a long, dark body that pushes the downtrend to a lower point
- Second Candlestick Bar
  Has a small body that gaps lower at the open
- Third Candlestick Bar
  Has a white body that gaps higher than the second candlestick bar and closes near the upper part of the first candlestick bar

On the other hand, an evening star consists of:

- First Candlestick Bar
  Has a long, white body that pushes the uptrend to a higher point
- Second Candlestick Bar
  Has a small body that gaps higher at the open
- Third Candlestick Bar
  Has a dark body that gaps lower than the second candlestick bar and closes near the lower part of the first candlestick bar

While these chart patterns could give you an insight into trends, they do not necessarily show the strength of the said trends. To measure this, traders make use of trendlines to analyze how different price points relate to one another depending on which kind of line will be formed: uptrend line, downtrend line, or horizontal line.

Take note that the conclusions that can be drawn through the use of trendlines are 100% accurate all the time. After all, there are plenty of gray areas in the market that could affect the validity of trendlines.

As a guide on how to tell if a trendline is valid or not, here are the three general rules about drawing trendlines:

1. A trendline must consist of three different price points.
   Going below this number would mean that you could basically draw a trendline anywhere in the chart.

2. The strength of the support or resistance of a particular trendline increases the more it gets touched.
   If a break of a trendline has been tested multiple times, then it can be said that there is a major shift in the trend.

3. A trendline becomes more meaningful the longer it gets.
   The length of a trendline is measured by time. This means that the true staying power of a trend is reflected by how long that trend has been going on.

Now, let's go over how you could use trendlines to enhance your ability to make successful trades.

A. Uptrend Lines

An uptrend line is drawn by connecting multiple lows, thus forming a support area for the buyers. It tells the rate of ascent—measured in dollars per period of time—that has been maintained by the buyers for a particular duration. As such, some swing traders use uptrend lines to determine their entry points for long positions.

While uptrend lines should be drawn through the lows, remember not to overdo this. It is okay if some prices have slightly intersected with the line, as long as the majority stays above the trendline.

B. Downtrend Lines

A series of peaks may be connected together by a downtrend line to mark the resistance area for sellers. Much like uptrend lines, a downtrend line offers more meaningful insight the longer it is and the more prices have touched it.

Be cautious when interpreting this though because a trendline break does not automatically means that a new trend will begin. Therefore, you should not immediately buy or short just because you have noticed a break in the trendline.

C. Horizontal Lines
These lines occur when the support level or resistance level has no or little movement. More often than not, only when these levels are breached could a new trend be developed.

In swing trading, you will encounter horizontal lines in certain chart patterns, such as the horizontal resistance level of ascending triangles, and the horizontal trendlines of support or resistance in a Darvas box.

As you have learned in this chapter, charting the market requires you to learn how to recognize patterns and examine if the said patterns are valid or not. These patterns are useful in guiding how you swing trade, but in order to come up with a well-rounded analysis of the market, you must also apply technical indicators and use them along with the chart patterns.

The next chapter covers the various technical indicators that every swing trader should know.

Chapter 10: Applying Technical Indicators

Back before the introduction of trading software programs and websites that could calculate technical indicators, traders would try to figure them out through manual calculation. Fortunately, there are several resources now that offer this service, many of which are free to use.

Given this, the aim of this chapter is not to teach you how to calculate technical indicators. Instead, we are going to discuss the right inputs that you need to get the technical indicator that you need, as well as how you could apply that technical indicator to market charts. The succeeding chapter to this one will cover how to analyze charts by combining these elements.

Before going through the nitty-gritty parts of understanding technical indicators, here are seven important reminders that you should remember throughout this chapter:

1. Technical indicators cannot be simply applied to every type of price charts. For example, many amateur traders have a tendency of applying trending indicators to price charts even if they do not even know yet if the market is in a trend. As a result, they would get false

signals about price movements towards either a support level or resistance level.

In reality, those movements are just fluctuations in prices. They are not signaling the start of a new trend.

Applying non-trending indicators can also lead to disastrous results when they are applied to a chart depicting a market in a trend. Traders would get false signals indicating either extreme levels of shares being overbought or oversold in the market.

How could one differentiate a trending market from its non-trending counterpart?

There are two ways you could go about this—either eyeball the chart or apply a technical indicator, such as the ADX (average directional index).

Eyeballing a chart requires you to go through the series of highs and lows, and check out if a pattern exists. To spot an uptrend, there must be a series of higher highs and higher lows. Conversely, a downtrend is characterized by a series of lower highs and lower lows.

If you do not see either of these patterns, check if there is a clear support area or resistance area. In case you find one, then you are dealing with a non-trending chart or a security that is in a trading range.

If you cannot recognize either the series or the areas, then it is best to avoid dealing further with that chart or security.

Going to the ADX, this indicator is used by many to determine the strength of a trend. Here are the probable readings that you could get by applying this indicator using a 14-day duration:

- o 20 or below
  The given security is in a trading range.
- o Between 20 and 30
  This is an ambiguous reading so you should examine further the direction of the ADX to figure out if the security is in a trend or not. If it is rising, then it means that the security is trending, but if it is falling, then the security is likely entering or is already in a trading range.
- o 30 or higher

The security is trending.

2. Be careful when analyzing price swings. There are instances wherein technical indicators fail to recognize significant price swings, thus rendering them essentially meaningless. There are also times when a price swing is just reflecting a data error or an unverified rumor.

   Given these, traders should learn how to properly examine and judge price swings. You may also be able to better protect yourself from making mistakes by choosing indicators that do not incorporate data errors, as well as by using other technical tools such as chart patterns when making your analysis.

3. Take into account the volume as well. While it is alright to use price as a sole basis of an indicator, doing so would not tell you about the commitment of other traders. To determine more accurately whether a movement is meaningful or not, consider the volume of security rises or falls as well.

   Given this, experts recommend using at least one technical indicator that incorporates volume. Aside from commitment, analyzing the volume would also tell you more about the staying power of a particular trend.

4. The accuracy of a technical indicator does not reflect its value.
   As discussed earlier, there is no technical indicator that can be accurate all the time. There are certain occurrences that could completely throw them off, thus giving traders a false signal instead.

   A good example of this is a whipsaw. This pertains to violent price movements that inevitably happen every now and then.

   With that said, don't judge a technical indicator based on its accuracy alone. Instead of focusing on the fruitless task of finding the perfect indicator, improve your risk management system instead so that you would be better protected when you receive false signals.

5. Try to limit yourself to two to three indicators per chart.
   When using a trading software or website, you might be tempted to add as many indicators as you think you need because doing so can be done with just a click of the mouse. It may look like it

would make things a lot easier for you, but overdoing this could amplify the noise that could drown out the important pieces of information that you should be paying more attention to instead.

Furthermore, adding more indicators would reduce your chances of getting consistent signals. As a result, you might be led to think that you should not make any trades at all during that time.

Experts suggest limiting the number of indicators to three. Any more than that would not provide you insightful results.

6. Your inputs should match your time horizon.
   The time settings of almost all technical indicators may be adjusted according to the information you need out of them. For example, you can set the duration of a moving average to see changes in price within a short period of time. However, take note that the shorter the duration is, the more likely you would encounter whipsaws.

   On the other hand, setting a longer duration for the moving average might turn it to become unresponsive. Yes, it may produce around two to three signals for a given year, but that would not be useful for swing traders who need to make trades within the following week.

7. Look for divergences when doing technical analysis.
   Divergences occur when the crowd in the market believes one side has the upper hand when, in reality, the opposite is true. As such, they can be used by traders to signify entry or entry points with lower risks than usual.

   Using divergences leads to getting more accurate signals compared to most indicators. Even renowned technical analyst John Murphy declared that they can produce the strongest signals for traders.

   However, divergences can be quite hard to spot, even for trading software programs. After all, recognizing one would require the keen eyes and interpretative mind of an experienced trader.

With these reminders under your belt, let's proceed to the ways on how you could recognize major trending technical indicators.

There are so many trending indicators to choose from, but I personally recommend the following three because of how useful they are for swing traders: DMI (Directional Movement Index), Moving Averages, and MACD (Moving Average Convergence/Divergence).

A. Directional Movement Index
    This indicator is used to determine if a security is in a trend and if it is, the direction of the said trend. There are three DMI plots:

    o   +DMI (Positive Directional Movement Index)
        This is used to indicate the effectiveness of buyers in pushing the prices beyond the high of the previous day. A high reading means that the buyers are strong.

    o   −DMI (Negative Directional Movement Index)
        This shows the efficiency of sellers in pushing down the prices until they are under the low of the previous day. If you get a high reading, then it means that the sellers are strong.

    o   ADX (Average Directional Index)
        Traders use this to measure the strength of a trend by highlighting

the difference between the +DMI and −DMI.

Swing traders analyze the crossovers between the +DMI and −DMI and use those as signals for trading. For example, the control of shares belongs to the bulls if the +DMI crosses above the −DMI. But if the −DMI crosses above the +DMI, it means that the bears have gotten the control. If the +DMI and −DMI frequently cross over one another, then you may say that neither the bulls nor the bears have the upper hand.

To maximize what you could get in return for using DMI, follow these steps:

1. Use an ADX plot to confirm if a trend is already in place.
2. In case a trend exists, use either moving averages or MACD to make an entry to a trade.
3. Incorporate the direction of +DMI or −DMI.
4. When the +DMI or −DMI crosses over the other, exit that trade.

B. Moving Averages
   This is one of the most often used indicators by swing traders. Basically, it is

designed to find out the underlying trend in a set of price data. There are two types of moving averages that you could choose from: simple moving averages, and EMA (exponential moving averages)

- o Simple Moving Averages
  This shows the consensus price agreement within the predetermined length of the moving average. For example, if prices increase more than their 14-day average, then you may say that traders and other market participants believe that the value of a particular security is going above the average within the 14-day period.

- o Exponential Moving Averages
  While this also indicates the consensus price agreement within a particular period of time, EMA weighs historical prices in a different manner—that is, more recent price action has a heavier weight than the older ones. Given this, EMA is more responsive than the simple moving averages. Unfortunately, this also increases the likelihood of getting false signals.

No matter which type of moving averages you use, the most important thing to look out for is the slope. If the moving average is rising, then the slope is positive. Conversely, the slope is negative if the moving average is falling. In case that the moving average is flat, then the slope is zero.

Traders should always make trades according to the direction of the slope. You should buy a security if the slope of the said security is positive. However, if you want to short security, then its slope must be negative.

Take note that completely basing your trades on a moving average would not be enough to ensure success. In general, a moving average tells you if it is time to make an entry. It won't tell you how much you should invest in a particular position, nor will it tell you where your stop loss should be or where you will take profits.

To guide beginners like you on how to use moving averages for swing trading, here are two strategies that you should try doing:

- o   Using Slope Changes

1. Set your moving average length.
   If you are using a daily chart, a length of 18 days or lower is advisable.

2. Look for a security that in a trend using the ADX indicator. Go for one that is trending upwards.

3. Buy the security once the flat or negative slope of the moving average becomes positive.
   It is better to wait until the last 30 minutes of the market hours before doing this so that you would be sure that there won't any reversal in the slope change. If you are not watching the market intraday, then buy the security on the days after the slope change has occurred instead.

4. Place your stop loss under the low of the day.

5. When the moving average becomes flat or negative again, exit that trade.

- o Using Moving Averages Crossovers
  1. Use the eyeball method or ADX to check if a trend exists.

  2. If there is, use either of the same methods to confirm if a moving average crossover is aligned with the direction of that trend.

  3. Once the short-term moving average crosses over the long-term moving average, buy the security.

  4. Place your stop loss level below a recent low.

  5. When the short-term moving average crosses under the long-term moving average, exit that security.

Using moving average crossovers allow swing traders to make earlier entries or exits compared to when they use slope changes. However, this added speed would open you up to more frequent occurrences of whipsaws so be extra careful when following this strategy.

C. Moving Average Convergence/Divergence

This bears similarities with the previous tending indicator. However, MACD has the added function of being able to tell not only the direction but also the intensity and strength of the buyers and sellers.

Generally speaking, MACD lines move according to the difference between the 12-day EMA and the 26-day EMA.

- The MACD line crosses above 0 if the shorter EMA crosses above the longer EMA.
- The MACD line crosses under 0 if the longer EMA crosses above the shorter EMA.

A moving average is also directly applied to the MACD, thus making it like the average of an average. A histogram is used to show the difference between the two.

- The strength of buyers is increasing if the histogram is rising.
- If the histogram is falling, then the sellers are becoming stronger.

Let's now discuss the three different trading signals that could be generated through the MACD:

a. Positive and Negative Divergences
    If a security reached a new low but this movement is not reflected in the MACD histogram, then a positive divergence has occurred. This means that the strength of sellers is decreasing, and you may expect a change in trend soon.

    Similarly, if the MACD histogram did not reflect a security's new high, then a negative divergence has developed. In this case, the buyers are losing their strength, and a trend change will happen in the near future.

b. MACD Crossing Over Its Nine-Day Moving Average
    Assuming that the market is in a trend, a buying signal is produced when the MACD Line crosses above the moving average. However, if the crossover happens below the moving average, then a selling signal will be generated.

c. MACD Line Crossing on Top or Under the 0 Line

The results you will generate from this is just similar to what you get by basing your trades on the crossover of the 12-day EMA and 26-day EMA. This means that you would not exactly benefit from the advantages of MACD, so it is better to refer to the previous two trading signals.

Now, let's move on to the major non-trending indicators. Also known as oscillators, these are used to monitor the price swings in trading ranges.

More often than not, securities are in trading ranges. At this point, neither buyers nor sellers can make significant moves to push the prices. Buyers are in their support area, while sellers are in the resistance area, so a party's attempts to push prices to their favor are frequently rebuffed by the other party.

The non-trending indicators are grouped between the overbought and the oversold securities. Of these, there are two that are quite popular among swing traders: stochastics, and RSI (Relative Strength Index).

A. Stochastics

This indicator is designed to compute the position of the day's close relative to a particular range that has been established over the specified period of time by the user. Basically, a security is overbought if the day's close is higher than the range.

If a security is overbought, then there is a bigger chance that it will revert to its mean. Keep in mind that this does not mean that this expected change will occur immediately.

Stochastics are composed of the following:
- o %K Plot
  This is used to show where the current close is in relation to the highest high and lowest of a security's price within a specified period. Most swing traders use a 14-day period for stochastics.

- o %D Plot
  This indicates the average of the %K plot for the past three days.

Stochastics primarily generates two types of signals:

  a. Positive and Negative Divergences

If the price of security falls to a new low but the stochastics indicator follows a higher trough, then a positive divergence has formed. This indicates that buyers are getting ready to push the prices while the sellers are exhausted.

On the other hand, a negative divergence occurs when the security prices have reached a new high but the stochastics indicator is found tracing a lower high. In this scenario, the buyers are the ones who are exhausted, and the sellers are preparing to push down the prices.

To use stochastics, follow these steps:
1. Check if there is an existing trading range with the use of either the eyeball approach or the ADX.

2. If there is, buy after a positive divergence has occurred—or shortly after a negative divergence has formed.

If you are entering a long position, do it only when the %K turns up above the %D. In case of the %D has turned up above the %K, enter a short position instead.

b. Crossovers from above the overbought level or under the oversold level
Usually, charting programs measure overbought and oversold levels on an 80-20 basis. This means that if a price makes a move towards an extreme—whether it is the upper 20% or the lower % of the boundaries of the past price range—traders may expect this extreme to be reversed.

Inexperienced traders tend to buy securities that are in a trading range just because the stochastics is either overbought or oversold. Unfortunately, doing so would increase the occurrence of whipsaws.

The better trading strategy is to wait for the stochastics to exit the overbought or oversold level. More often than not, the stochastics will remain overbought or oversold for a longer period of time.

To use the overbought and oversold levels in trading, follow these steps:

1. Confirm the existence of a trading range through the use of the eyeball approach or the ADX.

2. Wait until %K has entered either the overbought or oversold level.
    If it is through the overbought zone, short the security, but if it through the oversold zone, buy that security.

3. Make your exit once stochastics has reached the opposite level, or after a certain number of days have passed, or after you have achieved your return target.

B. Relative Strength Index

This oscillator is designed to compare a security unto itself. Through this, you would be able to determine if the price of a security is overbought or oversold. RSI can also create chart patterns that may be used to predict the direction of a breakout.

RSI works by examining a security's price history within a specified period—usually within 14 days. A comparison will be drawn between the average gain that has been achieved during the up days and the average loss experienced during the down days. The indicator will then be determined through the ratio between the average gains and the average losses.

RSI readings range from 0 to 100. Anything that is higher than 70 signals an overbought territory, while anything below 30 indicates an oversold area.

Let's go over how you could use the RSI indicator for swing trading:

    a. Positive and Negative Divergences
        Divergences in RSI happens when there is a failure to confirm the new high or new low of a security's price.

As a rule, positive divergences should only be traded when RSI turns up. Conversely, if the RSI turns down, then negative divergences can be traded. Remember to check first if the trading range exists though.

b. RSI-Developed Chart Patterns Compared to trading based on overbought or oversold areas, referring to the RSI is considered to be the more reliable approach.

c. Turning Down or Turning Up This bears similarities with the process of using stochastics to trade overbought or oversold territories. Here are the steps on how to use these signals:

1. Verify the existence of a trading range using the eyeball technique or the ADX.

2. Wait for the RSI indicator to breach through either the overbought or oversold area. If the RSI enters the oversold area, you should buy the security. However, you should

short instead if the RSI enters the overbought area.

3. Make your exit once the return target has been achieved, or after the RSI has reached the zone on the opposite side, or after a predetermined number of days have passed.

Combining these technical indicators with chart patterns help enhance the accuracy of your swing trades. To do this, you must evaluate trades according to what the charts and the indicators are saying. Only when both charts and indicators are saying the same thing should you take a trade.

A more thorough discussion about using patterns and technical indicators to analyze charts before trading trades or trading ranges can be found in the next chapter.

Chapter 11: Should You Trade Trends or Trading Ranges?

Traders generally gain profits by trading trends, trading ranges, or both. Prices that persistently move up or down becomes a trend. It may last from a few days up to years. On the other hand, trading ranges are characterized by securities that move only within defined price levels.

A large portion of swing traders goes for strong trends only. After all, the profits earned from trends tend to be higher compared to trading ranges.

Trends are also easier to manage for most traders. During an uptrend, for instance, you are assured that the price of the security will rise consistently. Even if it falls, the drop is pretty much negligible.

If you enter a trend within just a few days after it has started, then you don't have to worry a lot about risks. However, if the trend you have entered has been going on for weeks or months, then you are likely entering when every else is preparing to get off.

The problem with trading trends is that it can be tough to recognize when a new trend has started, and when to exit when the trend is nearing its end. As a swing trader, the latter issue matters more because you have to make a somewhat quick decision about whether or not to treat the signals as genuine—not as urgent as day traders, but you must certainly be agile and sensitive enough to successfully pull off your exits.

In comparison, swing traders who engage with trading ranges normally have a higher win ratio than those who exclusively trade trends. Why? Because when trading ranges, your objectives for profit and risk are easier to identify.

In terms of profit objective, all you need to look at is the other end of the range. For example, if you plan to short a stock that is priced at $30 per share, your objective in order to earn a profit is to cover that short near $20 per share.

Risks in trading ranges can be established easily too. If you have bought near $30 per share, you should exit once the stock goes below $29.

The biggest risk you will face when trading ranges is when the security starts developing a new trend. What you want instead is for a range to continue as it is. Once a new trend begins, your chances of being on the right of it are quite small.

Given all these, which of the two should you trade? If you can't choose between trends and trading ranges, it advisable for you to try trading both?

The thing is, there is no universal answer to the first question. Ultimately, it depends on what you want to get out of trading, and how much you are willing to risk when making your trades.

As for trading both, experts suggest leaving that for more experienced traders. You may eventually go for it, but make it a priority to understand trends and trading ranges first.

Those who can trade both do enjoy more opportunities to take advantage of the market. So, to upgrade yourself as a swing trader, aim to master trading trends and trading rangers as well.

To get you started on this, let's go over the proper ways to trade trends.

The first thing to do is look for strong trends. As discussed in earlier chapters, traders may follow either the top down or bottom up approach. Meanwhile, the strength of a trend may be assessed through the eyeball technique or technical indicators, such as ADX or DMI.

Once you have found strong trends that are worth your time and effort, your next step is to identify when to enter that trend. Getting this wrong will expose you to one of the biggest risks faced by swing traders: buying or shorting when a trend is nearing its end.

According to professional trader Ian Woodward, those who do not care about this risk are like dogs who are chasing after cars. At a glance, it may seem like a fun thing to do, but in reality, it is a reckless and dangerous thing to do.

What can you do to minimize the chances of making this mistake? Some check out the daily list of stocks reported by reputable finance newspapers, while others rely on security programs that are designed to recognize new highs and new lows. Here are some more helpful strategies that you should consider:

- Enter upon receiving a genuine signal
  This may be based on a chart pattern or technical indicators. Usually, chart patterns are faster in giving out signals, but technical indicators are easier to interpret.

- Enter on a day of strength
  Wait for the stock to develop three consecutive bars that indicate falling highs. Your entry should be made on the next bar that has a higher high than the previous one.

- Enter on a day of weakness
  This works similarly to the one explained above, but instead of declining highs, wait for rising lows. Again, you should enter

the succeeding bar that has a lower low than the previous bar.

Having entered a trade, your next step is to manage your risk by establishing your exit level. This exact price depends on when you have made your entry. Here are the common types of exit mechanisms that swing traders use:

- Exit signal from a technical indicator
  This means you are going to exit a trade on the break that falls below a moving average, or upon a crossover of MACD

- Exit level based on price
  If you have entered a trade on a new peak, then you have to set an exit level that is in the trading range that the stock is coming from.

- Exit level based on time
  This means exiting a trade after a certain number of days have elapsed. Setting this exit level shows that the exit price is not that important for the trader.

Now that you understand better to trade trends, let's proceed with trading ranges.

In general, looking for a security in a trading range is a tougher feat to accomplish than finding one that has new highs or new lows. As such, many swing traders rely on oscillators or the non-trending technical indicators to conduct their search, and to analyze when to enter and exit that security.

When identifying securities in a trading range, you must also consider their strength. This quality depends on the following factors:

- Time
  Trading ranges that have existed for a long time upon discovery tend to continue going on for a longer period of time.

- Tests of Support and Resistance
  The support levels and resistance levels grow stronger the more times a security touches them.

- Flat Ranges
  This refers to how much a trading range looks like a rectangle. You should look for one that is as flat as possible because that indicates that the trading range is true. Avoid that do not have clearly defined support or resistance areas.

Entering a trading range should be done on a day of strength, or upon a technical signal, such as stochastics.

In terms of profit objective, the target is just the opposite side. For the risk level, it should be established just below the support level.

Now that you have learned about trends and ranges, which of the two do you think you would go for as a swing trader? Do you want to earn higher profits by riding trades? Or are you okay with earning smaller profits gained through the more stable trading ranges?

Each type of trading has its advantages and drawbacks, but whatever you choose, remember that there will always be some form of risk that you have to manage. As such, the following chapter focuses on guiding beginners like yourself on how to measure and manage the risks of swing trading.

Chapter 12: Managing Risks

One of the most critical factors that would determine whether or not you would succeed as a swing trader is your risk management system. For many, this entails limiting your investment for a particular security, and diversifying your portfolio.

The thing is, while those are important, managing risk also means the executing of orders given by the risk management system. More often than not, this factor is the one that many traders find to be tough to carry out. After all, in this case, you are your own worst enemy.

It certainly doesn't help that the nature of trading itself is quite deceptive. What you may believe at first to be true may turn out to be false upon more careful observation. If you fail to exercise caution, then you would end up losing a lot—if not everything that you have.

The goal of risk management is to minimize the losses that you might experience as a trader. This is a two-fold approach: first in the level of individual security, while the second is concerned with the portfolio-level risks.

In this chapter, we will cover the various risk management rules that swing traders should observe. By the end of it, you will also learn how to combine these rules into a risk management system that would work for you.

Having this doesn't mean that you will never suffer a loss in your trades though. Instead, it is a means of protecting you as much as possible from any mistakes you make or unexpected occurrences in the market.

We shall start by learning how to measure the riskiness of an individual stock.

First things first, here are the various factors that you need to consider in order to do your assessment:

- Beta of the Stock
  Beta refers to the risk of a given stock relative to the market. Institutional traders tend to pay more attention to this than individual traders. However, this is an important point to include in your examination because it provides insight into how volatile a stock is compared to the market.

  Take note that a stock's beta is not a fixed number. It may increase or decrease even in a span of a day.

  There is also no optimal beta that you should look for in a security. For example, a security that has a high beta could be attractive, but make to check out if trading would put you at a risk of losing your entire investment as well.

You don't have to automatically ignore stocks with high beta. However, you must be extra careful and allocate less of your money to that security in case you end up deciding to trade it in order to minimize the risks of its volatile nature.

- Liquidity of the Stock
  How easy it is to enter and exit a security indicates how frequently the shares of a security have been traded.

Though the liquidity of a stock does not matter much when it comes to entry since traders can wait for the right timing, its significance is highlighted more when it is time for an exit. Just imagine the trouble you would be facing if you have to exit as soon as possible, but you can't find a buyer—or if you are shorting, a seller.

So, how liquid must a security's shares be before you buy a stock? The answer depends on the size of your account. If your investment is $25,000, then the optimal stocks to invest in must be trading at least 100,000 shares each day.

Furthermore, the size of your position should not exceed 5% of the average volume of shares per day.

- Size of the Company
  Again, institutional traders pay more attention to this factor compared to individual traders. Still, you need to take this into account because the stocks of small companies tend to perform better than larger companies in the long run. However, their stocks are also more volatile so engaging with them would affect how you establish your stop loss levels.

- Share Price of the Company
  Large company stocks—or also referred to as large caps—have lower volatility than those from smaller companies. You might be wondering though how you could distinguish which one is a large cap and which one is the small cap.

  Traders compute for the market capitalization to determine the value of a company. This is computed by multiplying the price per share of the company by its total shares outstanding.

Companies may be classified into one of the following categories based on their market capitalization:

- o Large Cap
  Market Capitalization: $15,000,000,000 or higher

- o Mid Cap
  Market Capitalization: Between $1,000,000,000 and $15,000,000,000

- o Small Cap
  Market Capitalization: Between $300,000,000 and $1,000,000,000

- o Micro Cap
  Market Capitalization: Below $300,000,00

As explained earlier, the smaller the company is, the less liquid it is. As such, many professional traders make it as a rule for them not to trade stocks that are worth $10 per share.

Stocks from micro cap companies are more prone to becoming manipulated, for example, through rumors in trading forums or networks. Such rumors would likely not make any significant effect on a large cap company. But for those under the micro cap category, an unverified rumor could send their stocks through the roof. Therefore, swing traders are advised against trading stocks from small, unknown companies.

Once you have determined the amount of risk that a stock entails, you may refer to that information when planning out your risk management system for the individual stock level.

Your objective at this point is to ensure that none of your positions would ruin your portfolio. In comparison, portfolio-level risk management is all about preventing the accumulation of multiple small losses from annihilating your entire portfolio of investments.

Managing risk at an individual stock level is done through position sizing. To establish this, you must first get to know how you are willing to lose in case of a failed trade.

A lot of experienced swing traders set their tolerance level for each position at 0.25% to 2% of their overall capital.

Let's say that yours is at 0.75%. To compute for the amount of tolerable loss for you, just multiply your capital by 0.75%.

So, if your capital is $100,000, you are willing to lose $750 on a single position.

From here, you can proceed to set your position size. There are two ways to go about this:

- By a Certain Percent of Capital
  To do this, multiply the total worth of your account by a predetermined percentage level. Though the computation part is simple, the tricky part is establishing that percentage level. Here are some tips on how to determine if you need to set a small or large percentage for a particular position.
  - Small Percentage (2% to 4%)
    Choose this is the security has the following qualities:
    - The share price is $10 or below
    - Beta is above 2.0
    - Illiquid relative to your account size
    - Small cap
  - Large Percentage (4% to 8%)
    - The share price is above $10
    - Low beta
    - Liquid relative to your account size
    - Mid or large cap

Once you have chosen a percentage for yourself, establish your stop loss level next. Base this amount on your loss tolerance threshold.

Going by the same example earlier, your stop loss level should be at a price that would make a position loss to be of an equivalent amount to 0.75% of your overall capital.

- By Risk Level
  This is considered by trading experts as the more strategic way of setting your position size.

  Let's use again the earlier example. If you were to use this method, you will determine your position size based on your preferred exit level. To compute for your exit level, establish a key price level where you want to make your exit, and then use that as a reference to finalize your position size.

  The price level of your exit should reflect the amount that would signal you that trade is taking a bad turn. It is not enough to wait until the price falls to an obviously bad point. What you need is an earlier warning sign. Experts recommend using a previous swing low to serve as your stop loss level.

So, putting these elements together, you may compute for your position size by dividing the amount of capital that is at risk by the difference of the entry price and your stop loss level. If your capital at risk is $750 (or the 0.75% of $100,000 capital), while the entry price is at $845, thus making your stop loss level at $805, your position size is 18.75 shares—which you may round down to 18 shares to further reduce the risk and keep you within your loss threshold.

After determining your risk management mechanisms for the individual stock level, you may proceed to build your portfolio while also keeping the risks to a minimum.

Other than making bad trades yourself, there are various external factors that could destroy your portfolio. Such events are typically out of your control so the only thing you could do is to monitor the risk level of your portfolio and then put in place the mechanisms that would minimize the impact of those risks.

Experts suggest the following ways to develop your portfolio with minimal risks:

a. Follow the 7% rule.
    This basically means limiting the cumulative capital at risk from all your

positions to only 7% of your total capital. Through this, you will be assured that the total amount of capital that you could possibly lose in a single day is just 7% instead of all of your capital.

Traders usually choose to set the tolerable loss percentage between 0.25% and 2%. The ideal maximum percentage, however, is around 0.5% per position. With this, you would still be able to diversify your positions since it would allow you to hold at least 14 different positions. Remember, the fewer positions you hold, the higher the risk level becomes.

b. Diversify.
    As the popular saying goes, "Don't put all of your eggs in one basket." That sums up the main rationale behind this risk management rule.

    In trading, portfolio diversification means investing your capital in different securities, industry groups, or asset classes. By doing so, the losses of a position will likely be offset by the gains of the others.

Let's go over the three different ways you could do to properly diversify your portfolio:

a. By increasing the number of securities
    The most basic way to diversify your investments is by buying several securities. Experts suggest holding 10 to 20 securities at a time in order to benefit from your diversified portfolio.

    Having multiple securities is not as simple as it sounds though. In order to achieve true diversification, the securities must be from different companies that belong to different industry groups. It would be even better if you could also invest in securities from other countries as well.

    Take note that the more positions you have, the less time you could spend on keeping track of them, and thus affecting the returns you may expect your investments. Given these, try your best to observe the suggested 20-security maximum limit.

b. By being exposed to more industry groups

According to the founder of Investor's Business Daily, William O'Neil, about 30% to 40% of a security's return is influenced by the industry group it belongs to. Because of this, expert traders know that limiting their investments to only a couple of industry groups would significantly increase the risks that they might face.

You might be wondering though what these industry groups are. In general, the following are the primary sectors and industry groups that traders may invest on:

- o Consumer Discretionary
  - Automobiles
  - Retailers
- o Consumer Staples
  - Drug Retailing
  - Food Retailing
  - Household Products
- o Energy
- o Financials
- o Healthcare
- o Information Technology
- o Materials
  - Capital Goods

- Commercial Services
- Industrials
- Transportation
  - Telecommunications
  - Utilities

To clarify, industry groups may be classified under sectors. For example, energy services, energy products, and energy drilling are types of industry groups that all belong to the energy sector.

Make sure to include the number of sectors and industry groups that you are planning to invest in into your trading plan. Again, there is no magic number that works for all, but many traders aim for at least four different sectors or six different industry groups.

c. By exploring other asset classes Aside from securities, you should also consider other investment vehicles to further diversify your portfolio. Here are the two main vehicles that will allow you to expand to other asset classes:
  - Exchange Traded Funds (ETF)

Through these funds, you will be able to trade commodities, currencies, and stocks from other countries.

o American Depository Receipts (ADR)
If you are based in the US, this will give you access to trade with companies outside the country without having to go there. Having international securities in your portfolio will enhance the benefits that you may expect from diversification.

c. Combine long positions and short positions.
This strategy will reduce the standard deviation of returns from your portfolio compared to when all you have are completely long or short positions. In case of a major market rally or decline, you will remain protected since the gains from either the long or short positions will offset the losses from the others.

How should you decide on the ratio of long positions and short positions for your portfolio? The answer depends on the strength or weakness of the market.

For instance, if the overall market is in a strong bull condition, then the number of your short positions should not be more than 20% of your total portfolio. On the other hand, if it is a strong bear market, then the long positions should not exceed 20% of your total portfolio.

Another way to lessen the risk of having too many long or short positions in your portfolio is by trading other asset classes that are in a trend that is contrary to the stock market. For example, in a strong bull market, consider entering short positions that come from either the currency market or commodities.

Regardless of whatever you have decided about the number of securities you will hold at a single time, the type of asset classes that you will invest in, and the ratio of long positions and short positions in your portfolio, remember to record every decision point you have established in your trading journal. You might have thought of the best risk management strategies for yourself, but if it is not in written form that is easily accessible to you, then chances are, you will forget or ignore them in the future.

Chapter 13: Improving Your Trades Through Performance Evaluations

To enhance your skills as a swing trader, you must take the time to evaluate how well your trades have done on a regular basis. There are various ways to go about this, but all of the evaluation methods basically aim to determine the returns of your portfolio.

A performance evaluation of your trades is not as straightforward as it may seem at first. Several factors may complicate your calculations, for example, commissions, SEC fees, taxes, and other types of expenses. Cash deposits may also add another layer of complexity to the computation of your returns.

Since such factors are natural parts of the process, the only way to handle them is to take them into account when doing your calculations. In this chapter, we will discuss how exactly you are supposed to do this.

Let's start with the easiest scenario, wherein the account you started with has had no deposits or withdrawals, and its growth in value over time is only due to trading.

To compute for your total return, in this case, you have to divide the difference between the ending and beginning value by the beginning value.

Here's an example to better understand this formula.

By the end of the year 2019, the account value of Trader Sean is $95,850. During the first three months of the following year, he buys and sells stocks every few days. As such, by the last day of March 2020, his account value has grown to $105,910.

Within those three months, Sean did not make any deposits or withdrawals from his account. Furthermore, the ending value of his account reflects the commissions he had paid during that period. As for taxes, those are not reflected because he is using a tax-deferred account for his investments.

From these data points, we may be able to determine Sean's total return by, first, subtracting $95,850 from $105,910. The resulting amount—which is $10,060—must then be divided by the beginning value: $95,850. After this, you will learn that the total return that Sean gained from January to March 2020 is 10.49%.

While this formula is quick and easy to use, you would likely have to adjust it since most swing traders perform deposits and withdrawals from their accounts. As explained earlier, this simple total return formula just straight-up assumes that there is neither a deposit nor a withdrawal made.

To consider these account movements into your computations, you may try using either of the following: the time-weighted return method, or the money-weighted return method.

1. Time-Weighted Return Method
   This is used to calculate the returns of an account regardless of the timing of the

cash flow movements. Because of this, many consider this as the superior method between the two.

2. Money-Weighted Return Method
This uses a formula that determines the return based on the account's return and the added value caused by the timing of the cash flow movements.

Since time-weighted returns would provide you a clearer answer that is not distorted by any large cash flow movements into or out of the account, let's focus on learning how to apply this method.

A time-weighted return method is actually a three-step approach. I'll give you a rundown of what each step entails so that you could better understand how to apply this method to your account.

Step 1: Break down the time period.
First, you need to break down the time period according to the number of deposits and withdrawals that have been made within the said period. This is important because you need to calculate the returns for each discrete time period.

To use this value in calculating the returns, you need to add 1 into the number of actual cash flow movements.

For example, take a look at this summary of cash flow movements in Sean's account that has a starting balance of $50,000:

- o Account Value Before Deposit
  - $58,500
- o Deposit
  - Date: 3 February 2020
  - Amount: $5,000

- o Account Value Before Withdrawal
  - $61,300
- o Withdrawal
  - Date: 14 April 2020
  - Amount: $3,000

- o Account Value Before Deposit
  - $63,780
- o Deposit
  - Date: 16 June 2020
  - Amount: $9,000

- o Account Value Before Withdrawal
  - $72,290
- o Withdrawal
  - Date: 20 December 2020
  - Amount: $7,000

- o Ending Balance
  - Date: 31 December 2020

- Amount: $68,350

Since Sean has made 2 deposits and 2 withdrawals within the year 2020, the calculation of return has to be for five—not four—time periods, as listed below:

- o 1st Time Period
  1 January to 2 February

- o 2nd Time Period
  3 February to 13 April

- o 3rd Time Period
  14 April to 15 June

- o 4th Time Period
  16 June to 19 December

- o 5th Time Period
  20 December to 31 December

Step 2: Calculate the return for each time period.

To do this, simply apply the formula for the total return of accounts without any cash flow movement for each time period.

- o 1st Time Period
  Return: 17%

- o 2nd Time Period

Return: -3.46%

- ○ 3rd Time Period
  Return: 9.40%

- ○ 4th Time Period
  Return: 0.67%

- ○ 5th Time Period
  Return: 4.69%

These returns must be connected to one another through the method called chain-linking to finally determine the total return of the account for the given year.

Step 3: Chain-link the returns of each time period.

The formula for chain-linking the returns of each time period is:

(1 + Return of 1st Time Period) x (1 + Return of 2nd Time Period) x . . . (1 + Return of Nth Time Period) − 1 = Total Return

Take note that the return must be converted into decimal form before you could proceed with adding, subtracting, and multiplying the values. The resulting total return may be turned back to percentage form so that it would be easier to understand later on.

Applying this formula to Sean's account, the chain-linking equation would look like this:

$(1 + 0.17)$ x $(1 - 0.0346)$ x $(1 + 0.0940)$ + $(1 - 0.0067)$ x $(1 + 0.0469) - 1 = 0.285$ or 28.5%

Now that you know how to calculate the total return of an account, what you should do next is to compare it to a particular benchmark that could tell you if you are outperforming the market.

Traders may refer to the following major benchmarks to evaluate their performance:

- For Cap Growth
  - Large Cap: Russell 1000 Growth Index
  - Mid Cap: Russell Mid Cap Growth Index
  - Small Cap: Russell Small Cap Growth Index

- For Cap Core
  - Large Cap: Russell 1000 Core Index
  - Mid Cap: Russell Mid Cap Core Index

- o Small Cap: Russell Small Cap Core Index

- For Cap Value
  - o Large Cap: Russell 1000 Value Index
  - o Mid Cap: Russell Mid Cap Value Index
  - o Small Cap: Russell Small Cap Value Index

These indexes may be accessed for free through this link: www.ftserussell.com. You can also use international indexes as your benchmark. For example, the website of the Bank of New York provides several compilations of indexes that may be used to compare international stocks that are traded in the US.

If you also short securities, then the nine benchmarks have given above is not that applicable to you. Instead, establish an absolute return level to serve as your benchmark. Most swing traders set this at 15% per year.

Having identified the benchmark that you would like to use, you are now ready to compare your return for the given year versus the annual return of the benchmark you have selected. In case that you do not have information yet about your annual return, then you may use your monthly return instead.

How should you interpret the results of this comparison?

If your actual return is greater than the return of the benchmark, then you are outperforming the average return as indicated in the index you have chosen.

There are various probable reasons for this, such as:

- Using margin or leverage
- Using cash well even though the market is declining
- Trading securities with higher beta compared to the benchmark
- Adding real value, which is possible as you increase your skills as a swing trader

Knowing how well you did in comparison to the market, in general, should serve as a basis on how you evaluate your current trading plan. You don't have to make any changes to the plan if it is not really needed, especially when your total returns have outperformed the benchmark. However, it would not hurt you at all to revisit the trades that you have made, and try to spot areas that could be further improved.

The market is ever-changing so it is best to keep upgrading yourself wherever you can. It is important to remember though that revising your trading plan should not be done too often.

Only do so when there is a significant reason, like a concrete benefit or a probable solution for the problems you have noticed in your trades.

Making frequent changes to your plan would keep you from knowing if a certain plan is actually effective or not. After all, you cannot truly judge a trading plan with data from only a short period of time.

Trading experts suggest reviewing your plan at least once per month. Go through your trading journal, and revisit the trades that you have closed. Those are good indicators of whether or not you should make some adjustments to your strategy.

For example, if your trading plan resulted in returns that are less than the average returns stated in the benchmark, then try your best to search for a common denominator among all your losing positions. Once identified, you may then add or revise the rules stated in your trading plan in order to prevent similar losses in the future.

On the flip side, you should also review your wins to determine if there are any common points among them. Should there be any, consider if you need to add or revise your trading plan rules to incorporate what you have done right in those trades.

As a final note, keep in mind that no trading plan works 100% of the time. There has also never been an absolutely perfect swing trader.

Losses are inevitable parts of swing trading. As such, you should always be prepared to handle them.

Many good trading plans end up as a failure when the trader fails to take into account the volatile nature of the overall market. As a result, they end up setting unrealistic expectations for themselves. Keep yourself from becoming this kind of swing trader by staying grounded and sticking with your trading plan.